Joel Edson Rockwell

Scenes and Impressions Abroad

Vol. 1

Joel Edson Rockwell

Scenes and Impressions Abroad
Vol. 1

ISBN/EAN: 9783337419929

Printed in Europe, USA, Canada, Australia, Japan

Cover: Foto ©Andreas Hilbeck / pixelio.de

More available books at **www.hansebooks.com**

SCENES

AND

IMPRESSIONS

ABROAD.

BY THE

REV. J. E. ROCKWELL, D.D.

NEW YORK:
ROBERT CARTER & BROTHERS,
No. 530 BROADWAY.
1860.

Entered according to Act of Congress, in the year 1860, by
ROBERT CARTER AND BROTHERS,
In the Clerk's Office of the District Court of the United States for the Southern District of New York.

TO MY WIFE,

WHOSE SOCIETY WAS THE CHARM WHICH MADE THESE SCENES
DELIGHTFUL AND MEMORABLE;

TO MY PARENTS,

WHOSE INSTRUCTIONS AND COUNSELS HAVE EVER BEEN
WISE, FAITHFUL AND SAFE;

TO THE CENTRAL PRESBYTERIAN CHURCH OF BROOKLYN,

WHOSE SYMPATHY AND EARNEST CO-OPERATION HAVE MADE
MY WORK AS A PASTOR PLEASANT;

THIS VOLUME IS DEDICATED WITH EVERY FEELING OF
RESPECT AND AFFECTION BY

THE AUTHOR.

PREFACE.

The substance of these SCENES AND IMPRESSIONS ABROAD was presented in the form of a Series of Lectures, before the congregation to which it is my pleasure to minister, without a thought of giving to them any farther publicity. Unexpectedly they enlisted such attention and apparent interest, as that it became necessary to adjourn from my Lecture Room, where they were commenced, to the main Auditory of the Church, which place was filled every Wednesday evening for three months. Most of the Lectures were very fully reported in the columns of the *Transcript*, of this city, with kind and courteous notices of the course. At the request of many who heard them, or who had read the reports of them, and in whose judgment I have confidence, they have been revised and published in the form in which they now appear.

I have attempted nothing in these Lectures but a familiar and faithful description of a few of the more important features of the usual route of European tourists, presuming that a minute detail of some of the principal and most interesting sights, which might be taken as a sample of the whole, would be preferable to a more general and hence less definite description of all.

The reader will find here only the familiar utterances of one, who having returned from a pleasant journey, wishes to share, as far as possible, with his friends whom he left behind him, the pleasures which he has enjoyed. This rich field has been so often reaped, that the author can only hope to bring in a few gleanings. If here and there is found a sheaf or a flower that may be profitable or pleasant, his highest wishes will be met and satisfied.

Brooklyn, N. Y., Feb., 1860.

CONTENTS.

I.—OUTWARD BOUND.

A Sabbath at Sea — Icebergs — Sea Life — An Irish Pilot — Dieppe — Rouen — Church of St. Ouen — Notre Dame, page 27

II.—PARIS.

Philosophy — Historical — The Seine — The Tuileries — Obelisk of Luxor — Parisian Life — Bois De Boulogne — Bastile — St. Roch — The Madeline, ... 50

III.—CHURCHES AND PALACES OF PARIS.

Notre Dame — Imperial Cortege — St. Germain L'Auxerrois — St. Bartholomew's Eve — Sainte Chapelle — Versailles — Recollections — Galleries — A Sad Truth — Petite Trianon, 72

IV.—PARIS TO LYONS.

The Louvre — Hotel De Cluny — Fontainbleau — The American Consul at Lyons — Church of St. Ireneus — St. Jean — Silk Manufactories — Protestantism — Religious Liberty, . 87

CONTENTS.

V.—LYONS TO NAPLES.

Montalimar — Nismes and Arles — Bay of Naples — Getting Ashore — A Pleasant Ride — Pompeii — Amphitheatre — Tragic Theatre — Diomed — The Overthrow — Contrasts, . . 110

VI.—ROME.

Civita Vecchia — A Panorama — The Pope-Relics — The Capitol — The Bambino — Villa Albano, ... 135

VII.—ROME AND ITS CHURCHES.

"The Church at Rome" — Popery — Sights of Rome — St. Peter's — Statistical — Grandeur — Decorations — The Vatican — Illumination of St. Peter's — Babylon, . . . 157

VIII.—ROME TO FLORENCE.

Leaving Rome — A Night Passage — Leghorn — San Lorenzo — Medicean Chapel — Galileo — Miseracordia, . . 182

IX.—FLORENCE TO TURIN.

Beautiful Italy — The Papal Church — Genoa — Sardinia — Turin — Pignerol — La Tour — The Vaudois — Church of Copiès — Waldensian Worship — Historical, . . . 208

X.—THE ALPS.

Susa — Diligence Riding — An Alpine Pass — Lanslebourg — Geneva — Chillon — Cretins — Alpine Scenery — Sunrise at Chamouni — Mer De Glace — Crossing a Glacier — Forclaz — The Col De Balme — Interlaken, ... 235

XI. — THE RHINE.

Jungfrau — Staubbach — Berne — The Rigi — Lake Luzerne— Basle — Baden Baden — Conversation haus — Gambling — Basle Mayence — Rhine Boats — The Mouse Tower —Ehrenbreitstein — Cologne — Amsterdam — Rotterdam — Antwerp — Brussels — Waterloo, ... 267

XII. — ENGLAND.

Dover — An English Inn — London — Westminster Abbey — Houses of Parliament — The Temple — Business Haunts — The Tower — Zoological Gardens — Sydenham — British Museum — Hampton Court — Windsor Castle — Oxford — Stratford on Avon Kenilworth, ... 295

XIII. — SCOTLAND, IRELAND, HOME.

Scottish Scenery — Melrose Abbey — Edinburgh — Holyrood — John Knox — St. Giles' Church — The Castle — Arthur's Seat — The Sabbath — Sterling Castle — The Trossachs — Loch Lomond — Glasgow — Dumfries — A Scotch Welcome — Liverpool — Dublin — Cork — Queenstown — An Irish Jaunting Car — Homeward Bound — A Storm at Sea — A Night in a Gale — Sea Amusements — Home Again, ... 340

SCENES AND IMPRESSIONS ABROAD.

I.

OUTWARD BOUND.

IT is my purpose, as far as possible, to reproduce the scenes through which it has been my pleasure to pass during my absence from home in search of health—for the entire restoration of which I desire here to render my thanks to that God who has watched over us while we have been absent one from another. It is my sincere wish that you may enjoy with me, the journey which I have accomplished; and to this end I propose, in a series of familiar lectures, to bring before you, as distinctly as I may be able, the lands which I have visited and the impressions I have received. When I found my health rapidly giving way, after eighteen years of ministerial labor, one half of which has been devoted to this church, you kindly and cheerfully assented to my request for leave of absence; and on the 7th of May, in company with my wife and a mutual friend, we left in the steamer *City of Washington*, Captain Petrie, for Liverpool. A crowd of friends were present to bid us farewell, and, as the noble vessel swung away from her moorings, waved us their kind adieus. The ship's cannon thundered forth their rough salute, which was answered by echoes from the shore. We felt that we were afloat, and every moment separating more and more widely from all we loved and held dear. At Sandy Hook we parted with our pilot, by whom we sent messages home, and were soon rocking upon the restless waves of the open sea.

Sabbath, May 8.—Rose early to breathe the fresh and invigorating air of the morning. One must be hopelessly an invalid who could not drink in health with this fresh and bracing breeze that is bearing us onward thus rapidly along the great highway of the ocean. At half past ten the bell tolled for the regular Sabbath service. The passengers were gathered upon the quarter-deck, occupying seats which had been prepared for them, while the crew, in their neat blue jackets, filled the boats that were swung upon either side. A capstan, neatly draped with flags, served for a pulpit, which, at the request of Captain Petrie, I occupied.

In accordance with the regulations of the New York, Philadelphia and Liverpool Steamship Company, I read the Service of the Church of England, adding, in the prayer for the Queen, the name of the President of the United States. The subject of my discourse was, "The Christian Hope, the Anchor to the Soul." Drawing my illustrations as much as possible from the sea, I endeavored, I think with some success, to enlist the attention and interest of the sailors. It was a novel and pleasant scene, that hour of worship in the open air, upon the deck of a vessel that was plowing its way through the ocean. And it was a delightful thought, that the same God who was listening to the worship of loved ones at home, and of tens of thousands who were gathered in solemn temples to praise His name, was also upon the sea, ready and willing to hear the prayers of His people, and to accept the tribute of their thanks.

At 12 o'clock our position was found to be lat. 40° 21', long. 68° 31'; distance run 255 miles. Monday, 9th, lat. 41° 46', long. 62° 50'; distance run, 271 miles. The weather is hazy, but clear enough to give us our first view of a whale, whose presence is indicated by the water which he occasionally throws up in a jet, and which descends in a shower of spray.

Tuesday, 10*th*.—Lat. 43° 21', long. 58° 21'; distance run, 230 miles. Passed a vessel homeward bound, and as we thought of the fair land that would soon open upon her crew, we could not but repeat the words we had so often heard amid the songs of youth:

> "While the waves are round me breaking
> As I pace the deck alone,
> And my eye in vain is seeking
> Some green leaf to rest upon ;

> What would I not give to wander
> Where my loved companions dwell?
> Absence makes the heart grow fonder:
> Isle of beauty, fare thee well."

Wednesday, 11*th*.—Lat. 46° 17', long. 53° 55'; distance run, 237 miles. To-day we obtained our first view of those wonderful gifts of the Polar regions, "icebergs." The sea was as calm as a lake, and the sky clear and cloudless. Far in the distance was seen a bright and glittering object, which, as we neared it, proved to be one of those unwelcome visitants of the American waters, which, being formed far up amid the sea of ice which surrounds the Polar circle, are broken off in vast masses from their native glaciers, and, by the action of the winds and the waves, floated down towards the warmer regions of the south, when, after too often putting in jeopardy the life of the sailor, they are gradually dissolved and disappear. As they melt away, they assume an almost endless variety of shapes, and, when seen at a distance, might be taken for castles, and ships, and churches, or cottages. Some of them are of great extent, and are exceedingly dangerous neighbors, when, as was the case with us, they appear during a fog. The cry, "Hard a' port," early one morning, brought those of us who were up to the deck, just in time to see one of them float by us, near enough to have leaped upon it.

In the course of the day fourteen icebergs were in sight, one of them being of immense extent. Towards evening we passed Cape Race, and signalized the station, in the hope that our passage thus far might be communicated to our friends at home. Just at sunset we caught sight of the harbor of St. John's, ten miles distant, the last land we shall see until we sight the shores of Ireland.

Thursday, 12*th*.—Lat. 49° 14′, long. 49° 9′ ; distance run, 254 miles. As there is nothing of especial interest, except looking out upon a boundless ocean, we may as well take a general view of sea life. Our company is large and pleasant, consisting of over 100 cabin and 200 steerage passengers, with a captain who knows how to sail a ship and to make his passengers comfortable and happy. When off duty he has a kind word for all. His officers are quiet and gentlemanly, and his crew orderly and well-behaved. The chief amusement on ship-board is eating and drinking. Breakfast at 9, lunch at 12, dinner at 4, tea at 7, and supper at 10. The hours are divided into watches, indicated by bells every half hour. The first watch beginning at 4 and ending at 8; the second from 8 to 12; the third from 12 to 4; and the dog watch from 4 to 6 and from 6 to 8. At eight bells, which indicates the commencement of a new watch, the officers and hands on duty retire, and the boatswain's whistle calls the sleepers to their posts; the boatswain, in this case, being of the most conventional order, a fat and jolly old sea-dog, who rolls over the deck, and sports his silver whistle with the most evident pride and satisfaction, and gives to its notes a flourish which only an old salt can appreciate. At 9 o'clock observations are made for latitude, and at 12 the longitude is taken, after which the result is posted upon the bulletin, and day by day we are thus able to map down our place upon the ocean. There is a good library on board, which serves to while away our leisure hours.

Friday, 13th.—Lat. 51° 11′, long. 42° 45′. Distance, 275 miles. Wind W. N. W., increasing, and the ship rolling heavily. Found it necessary to use guards at table.

Saturday, 14th.—Lat. 51° 12′, long. 35° 25′. Distance, 277 miles. Lightning and cloudy, with fresh breeze.

Sunday, 15th.—Lat. 51° 11, long. 27° 40′. Distance, 295 miles. Preached from the text, "How shall we escape if we neglect so great salvation?"

We held also a service in the steerage amid a large and attentive audience.

It was pleasant to meet there a Christian friend who had provided himself with a bundle of tracts, published by the *Presbyterian Board*, and to see here and there persons engaged with evident interest and seriousness in reading these little messengers of mercy.

Monday, 16th.—Lat. 51° 14′, long. 18° 58′. Distance, 293 miles.

Tuesday, 17th.—Lat. 51° 53, long. 12° 47'. Distance, 272 miles. Obtained our first sight of the Irish coast at 6 P. M. The long twilights are a marked feature of our high Northern latitude. At 9 o'clock in the evening there was still sufficient of daylight to enable me to make an entry in my note-book, which was written off the Skellig Rocks, making for Cape Clear 50 miles distant.

Wednesday, May 18th.—At 5 o'clock A. M. took on board an Irish pilot off the Old Head of Kinsail. He was a rare specimen,—coming on board in a dress which might have been new once, but at a very distant period. As we were anxious to hear the news from Europe, we asked if he had any papers. He said, "Yes, but they were a week old, and had gone ashore in the boat." We asked if he had any news of the War. He said "he believed war or peace had been declared, but he could not tell which." The Irish coast is one of exceeding beauty, basaltic in formation, and presenting to the eye a pleasing variety of bold head-lands, green fields and castled hills. At Queenstown harbor we got from the steamer which took off passengers for Cork, the first news of the war.

Thursday, 19*th.*—Sailed up the channel and the Mersey, and arrived at Liverpool at 12 o'clock, just five hours less than 12 days from New York.

Passing rapidly on towards Paris, we stopped a day in London, intending to take England in our route home. Taking the train of the South Western Railway, we reached New Haven in a few hours, and after 6 hours' sail in a pretty little channel-steamer, we landed at Dieppe, and were taken in charge by two *gensdarmes,* who conducted us to the *Bureau du Paquebot,* where our passports were *visé,* and we received permission to land and to proceed on our journey to Paris, and through France.

Dieppe is an ancient Norman city of 20,000 souls, inhabited by rough, independent and hardy fishermen, who find the shores of France, and their neighborhood, well fitted for their peculiar business. In summer it is also a favorite watering-place of the French, and splendid hotels have sprung up which give to the town an appearance of growth, life, and activity, quite American. The approach to Dieppe is exceedingly picturesque. The shore for many miles is lined with white cliffs, often rising to a great height. Just here these high walls have been sundered and a fine harbor is formed, in which a large fleet may find safety.

The city has a quaint and odd look to an American. It has an ancient cathedral, built in the old Norman style, and which was preserved from conflagration during the English invasions by setting fire to some straw upon its roof, giving the English troops the idea that its destruction was accomplished, and turning their fire to another quarter. Upon the sea-shore, looking down a beautiful and bold coast, are large hotels, arranged in the taste so natural to the French, and with all the appliances for fashionable amusement and dissipation. The port is spacious, and has a fine castle and citadel.

We take a stroll along the shore, and are amused with the dress of the fishermen and women, who preserve to a great extent the old Norman fashions, and whose whole appearance is to an American, an entire novelty, and makes him feel that he is in a strange land.

Leaving Dieppe in the afternoon we pass on towards Rouen, by railway, through a beautiful country, well cultivated, and covered with flower-gardens; and reach that ancient city just as the night has closed upon us. We had been directed to a hotel where English was spoken, and found ourselves in a quiet and cozy old French inn, where our only interpreter soon left us to the care of the hostess, who, though very pretty and agreeable, was unable to speak a word of English. Of course all our knowledge of French had to be summoned to our aid. Rooms were to be provided, tea to be had, bills to be made out, servants to be summoned, and the waiters to be talked to in *French*.

There is nothing like being cornered, to bring out one's resources; and we found our old hours with Ollendorff and others, returning to us most advantageously. Our first attempt at French was so far successful that we found ourselves in possession of all the comforts the inn could afford.

Rouen, the ancient capital of Normandy, has now about 90,000 population. It lies upon the Seine, which is here navigable to steamers and small ships.

Ptolemy, in the second century, mentions this city. When Rome had subjugated France, it became a military post of considerable importance. The Frank succeeded the Romans in its possession; then the Norman pirates took it in 841, and have left the characteristics of their nation all over the city. Rouen suffered repeated sieges, and at length fell to France, to whom it now belongs. During the Reformation, that work found many friends here; and in the massacre of St. Bartholomew, 500 of its families perished under the cruel mandate of the Popish authorities. At the time of the Revolution it again became the scene of terrible butchery, when 1,200 persons perished by the guillotine. Rouen, although a large and important city, has, from the great age of its buildings, an appearance of dilapidation which really belies its actual condition. It is an important manufacturing town, lying upon the direct route from Paris to Havre and Dieppe. But its streets are narrow and compact. A fine boulevard passes four miles around the site of its old wall, filled with beautiful trees, which somewhat relieve its antique grandeur with what is new and cheerful. But everything about tells the story of its age. Its houses are quaint and rickety, with curious ornamental carvings, and images of saints, and martyrs, and Virgin Marys. At every turn some relic of antiquity meets you. Here is a mutilated statue of a saint, and there a Gothic fountain. Grotesque heads grin at you from many a door-post and window-frame. Fanciful flowers, the like of which were never seen, are carved in queer and stiff festoons around many a decaying mansion. Hobgoblins and apostles, wolves' heads and headless martyrs, serpents and wily priests, in stiff and stately stone, look out upon you from many a crumbling buttress and mouldering tower. In the market-place, surrounded by strange-looking buildings, stands the statue of Joan of Arc, the Maid of Orleans, who, for her wonderful control over the army of her native land, was burned as a witch, by the English, in 1431, upon the spot where her statue now stands.

But the great features of the city of Rouen are its two splendid churches, which present to us some of the finest specimens of Gothic architecture to be found in Europe. We visit first the church of St. Ouen, founded in the year 533. In 844, it was burned during the Norman invasion. In the year 1303, the first stone of the present structure was laid. As you approach it you notice the elaborate carvings upon the casements of the doors, representing, in bas-relief, scripture scenes and history. Over the windows, and upon the pillars, and under the eaves, start out those strange and grotesque figures which form a part of the ancient Gothic style. On entering, you are struck with awe and wonder. Before you lies a vast pile, 450 feet long by 100 feet high, and about the same in width. The ceiling, sustained by huge clustered columns, rises from the stone floor, on which appears no pew or seat to break in upon the perfect proportions of the interior. Eleven chapels surround the choir, in all of which service is held at different times; and while in one part of the edifice a congregation is listening to preaching, in adjoining chapels mass and other services are performed, with no danger of interfering, the one with the other.

The church is lighted by 125 immense windows of stained glass; and when we pass into the last chancel, and look up to the vast ceiling, rising to the height of 100 feet, and through the arches, columns, statues, paintings and windows, that make up this splendid pile, the effect is overwhelming.

Passing out and paying a franc to the sexton, and followed by one of the swarms of guides that offer to show us the city, we visit the cathedral of Notre Dame, where new wonders await us. There was a chapel here in the ninth century, a part of which still remains. In the year 841 it was pillaged, but not destroyed; enlarged in the tenth century; and in 1117 struck by lightning, and burned in 1200.

The present cathedral is the work of three separate ages, each style being distinctly defined. Its length is 418 feet, its greatest breadth 100 feet, and the height of the nave 96 feet. It has three principal towers. The tower of St. Roman is the oldest,—230 feet high. Next comes the "Tour de Beurre," or Butter Tower, 230 feet high, built by the granting of indulgences to eat butter in Lent. The third tower, which is to be 436 feet high, is built of iron, and will soon be finished. The walls and doors and windows are ornamented with the most grotesque and elaborate carvings of saints and scripture scenes. As we enter, we are again astonished with the vision of majestic beauty and grandeur that meets our eye. Wherever we turn we behold something to elicit our admiration, or to fill us with wonder. The light streams down through the stained Gothic windows upon twenty-five chapels which surround the choir, and which are filled with splendid paintings, with fine statuary, and with the monumental relics of past ages. Here we meet with the first specimens of painted bronze, dating back to the year 994. Here, in stiff and stately grandeur, lie the mighty dead.

Here, Richard "Cœur de Lion" has his tomb; and William "the Long Sword," and Rollo, first Duke of Normandy; and many a noble name is recalled as we pass the sepulchres that are placed around the building, in almost every chapel.

Such was the effect of this first sight of truly Gothic grandeur, that even now, after having looked over the most famous churches of Europe, I still find myself recalling this vast and splendid edifice as one of the wonders of France.

One is lost in feelings of awe, as he stands and looks over this magnificent Gothic pile, and hears the solemn music of the organ and the chant of the robed priests; while the cries and noises of the city without,—the rumbling of wheels, and the hurry of active life,—present, in strange contrast, the world and the church—the worship of Mammon and of God.

As a picturesque city, Rouen is one of the most remarkable in France:—full of strange contrasts; odd and antique costumes of past centuries perpetuated from age to age; fine modern mansions and quaint old tumble-down houses, scarcely fit for cattle; splendid relics of old churches used now as rag-shops, or warehouses, or for whatever they can be rented, closed for religious purposes since the Revolution; and of the few which remain, many a sad mark of the spoiler's hand being left by the Protestants, in their zeal, at the Reformation. In short, no one should go to Paris without spending a day or two at Rouen.

Leaving it in the afternoon, a ride of four hours brings us to the wall of Paris, 85 miles distant. And now evening is coming on, we have only time to get comfortably settled at our hotel "de Lille et d'Albion," where we will meet you next week for a sight of Paris.

II.

PARIS.

IT was on a bright and beautiful afternoon in May, when the shrill whistle of the locomotive announced our approach to the city of Paris. In a few moments we had passed through its walls and were at the railroad station, undergoing the usual examination of baggage, to discover if any contraband articles were about to be smuggled into the city. This, with the constant inspection of the passport, is a nuisance which the American notices first and most frequently in Europe, and to which it is almost impossible to become accustomed. But the traveller should take the annoyance good-naturedly, remembering that it is not the fault of the custom-house officers, who but do their duty, and usually do it as gentlemen. His best way is to treat them politely—have his keys and passport always ready—and he will escape with comparatively little trouble. Let him avoid all irritation or anxiety, and he will find the examination will be but a mere form. A hand will be thrust down here and there in his baggage, and then his keys returned to him with a courteous bow, and he permitted to go on his way; while the man who allows himself to get worried and irritated, will find his troubles increasing with every stage of his journey.

I found in my own experience a good deal of virtue in a bit of practical philosophy, which I learned from my friend Mr. Smith, on our voyage to Europe. It was the story of a jolly tar who had been promoted from the forecastle to the cabin, and from hauling ropes and reefing sails, to waiting on the table.

In his first essay at his new business, he got along well enough, until he came to a lady who did not wish soup. "Take it away," said she, "I don't wish it." "Oh, but you must have it, you must have it, ma'am," replied Jack, "it's the rules of the sarvice." So I remembered that the passport system and the custom-house search were "the rules of the sarvice," a part of the penalties one paid for travelling; and I acted accordingly, and never had the slightest difficulty, except once, in Prussia, where an official found a small doll in my trunk. The soldier took the toy to his superior officer, who only gave one look at it, with an indescribable shrug of the shoulders, and exclaimed "bon" —all right.

Taking a carriage at the depot, we were soon set down at the Hotel de Lille et d'Albion, and were saluted with a profound French courtesy by the hostess, and in a few moments conducted to our rooms overlooking a neat garden full of flowers and statuary, and giving us just the slightest peep into the Rue de Rivoli and the gardens of the Tuileries. As the evening is upon us, we have only time to walk out into the nearest boulevard, where we stumble upon two friends whom we have not seen for years, and to return to our rooms and look over a little of the history of Paris, and to study somewhat its topography and statistics.

There was a rude settlement upon the island in the Seine when Julius Cæsar invaded Gaul. The people who dwelt here were a fierce and hardy race of hunters and fishermen. Their worship was Druidical, which was in time succeeded by Roman idolatry, traces of which are still found over the city.

Constantine honored the place with a visit, and Julian spent a winter here.

At the close of the fifth century, Clovis routed the Romans and made himself master of Paris. Then he married Clotilde, embraced Christianity, and built a church. The introduction of the Christian religion, according to the monkish tradition, was accomplished by St. Denis, A. D. 250. He was beheaded at Montmartre, and his headless statue adorns the porch of the church of St. Germain l'Auxerrois, whither he walked after his execution, with his head in his hands.

Towards the middle of the fourth century the growing wealth of Paris excited the cupidity of the Normans, who sacked and burnt it. After the rise of the Capetian kings, the city began to increase and flourish. Century after century has witnessed its growing wealth and splendor. Revolution after revolution has passed over it, only to leave new monuments of taste and luxury, and to hand down to other generations some new leaf in the history of the metropolis of France.

Paris now contains 1,250,000 souls, of whom about one half are working people. There is annually expended $48,000,000 for food, $70,000,000 for dress, and $10,000,000 for wines. There are about 3,000 liquor dealers in Paris, while in our two cities there are probably 8,000, —a strange disproportion in favor of the French metropolis, where I saw less drunkenness in a fortnight than one may see here in a single hour.

But let us turn from these historical notices and statistics to begin our rambles over the city. Walking from our hotel, which lies hard by the Palace of the Emperor, and crossing the garden of the Tuileries, we come to the banks of the Seine, which flows through the city from the south-east to the north-west, dividing it into two unequal parts. Like most of the rivers of

Europe, which are rendered important by their historical connections chiefly, an American feels a sense of disappointment when he finds here a small and insignificant stream. It is crossed by a multitude of bridges, and navigated by small canal-boats, which bring down produce from the country.

All along the banks of the Seine are swimming-schools and bath-houses. But when one looks at the muddy stream that is hurrying along towards the sea, holding in solution the soil of the country and the filth of the city, he wonders how a Frenchman can ever get clean there.

There are twenty-three bridges across the Seine, four of which are built of iron, one of wood, and the rest are substantial structures of stone: of these the Pont-Neuf is the most celebrated.

Along the banks of the river are beautiful quays, extending in all more than eleven miles. They present the appearance of large terraces, with fine M'Adamized roads and foot pavement, bordered with trees neatly trimmed and kept in perfect order. Benches are placed along the route for tired pedestrians, and in the evening the whole is brilliantly lighted with gas, thus furnishing a magnificent promenade for the citizens of Paris.

But the grand resort of the Parisians begins with the garden of the Tuileries, where hundreds of seats are let every afternoon, by persons employed for the purpose, and extends upward as far as the Arc de Triomphe, near the city walls.

Besides these splendid grounds, to which we shall recur again, are the Boulevards, which are fine streets, well shaded by trees, and extending almost around the city. There may be met of an afternoon tens of thousands, looking into the gay shops which are filled with articles of taste and use, or sitting down before a restaurant enjoying an ice, or a bottle of wine, with a group of friends.

When we add to these general features the splendid churches; palaces which appear in almost every part of the city, each of which has its thrilling story of the mighty past; the monuments which rise from every elevation and square;

the fountains that play in the sunlight, or shine in their softened beauty amid the lamps that make Paris so brilliant at evening; with the parks, and statues, and military and civil establishments of the city, we have some idea of what we are to see in passing through the gay capital of France. Beginning now with the garden of the Tuileries, after we have looked at the long lines of statuary, and the fountains and groves which adorn the palace grounds, we turn our faces westward, and take our first walk of exploration.

Entering a dense grove filled with chairs to rent, we come upon two hemicycles of white marble, with small and tasteful enclosures in front, adorned with some pieces of fine statuary. These are relics of the Revolution, and were designed by Robespierre.

Passing onward, we come to two piers which rise into solid walls, from the west barrier of the Tuileries, enclosing a fountain and some groups of statuary designed to represent the great rivers of the old world.

Leaving the gardens by the western gate,

which is always guarded by sentinels, we come into a vast circle called the Place de Concorde. Until the time of Louis XV., this spot was a useless and shapeless piece of ground. It is now enclosed by balustrades, upon which stand eight colossal statues, which represent the chief cities of France. In the centre, and upon the very spot where the unfortunate Marie Antoinette died by the guillotine, stands the celebrated obelisk taken from the ruins of Luxor, and covered with hieroglyphics, supposed to have been wrought during the time of Sesostris. This obelisk was brought from Egypt at a great expense, and its mate is to be found at Rome. A story is told about the obelisk at Rome which is worth repeating. Workmen were engaged in raising that massive piece of stone to the pedestal prepared to receive it, and strict orders had been given that, during the operation, no one of the vast multitude assembled to witness it should utter a word. Gradually the ponderous stone rose very nearly to its place, and then it refused to move any farther. The ropes were stretched to their utmost tension, and there was great danger that the vast slab would fall, when suddenly an English sailor cried out, "Wet the ropes." The man was immediately arrested, but the quick ear of the foreman had caught the magic word. The ropes were wetted—they contracted—and the obelisk rose to its place. The next morning the sailor was not only released, but was most liberally rewarded. This is one of the instances in which apparent impossibilities have been achieved by a little practical knowledge.

On either side of the column stands a fountain; the one is dedicated to the ocean and the other to the river. They consist of circular basins fifty feet in diameter, on which are erected colossal figures, with various emblems of the Ocean, Commerce, Art, and Science. Passing through the Place de Concorde, we come to the Champs Elysees, which is a long and beautiful park adorned with statues, and fountains, and groves.

There stands the Palace of Industry, an immense building designed as a place for the exhibition of works of art. Taking our way through a magnificent avenue, we come to the

Arc de Triomphe, built at an immense expense by Napoleon I. It is 152 feet high by 137 broad, and 68 deep; and is adorned with representations of the great battles of the Empire.

Here, in these Elysian fields, is the great resort of the gay citizens of Paris. Yonder, an avenue leads to the famous, or rather the infamous, Chateau des Fleurs. Here are given balls and concerts, attended by persons whose reputation is by no means doubtful. I did not enter the place, although I was informed that it was fitted up in a style of Oriental splendor. But when I saw carriages driving up to the entrance, some filled with young men, and others with females, who were to meet them amid these fascinations and excitements, I felt that over the portals of that place might be written the words of the wise man: "Her steps take hold on hell!" And these, I fear, are the resorts with which many a young American is familiar, who is sent to Paris to *finish* his education. For my own part, I would rather send a youth to the State Prison to perfect his morals, than to this city. There is doubtless a great deal of science in its schools, and one may learn French perfectly, and gain a certain degree of polish, but he is in danger of acquiring much, of which he might better have remained ignorant for life. Every thing really useful to a young man may be acquired as readily at home, and with much greater safety. In Paris, where vice is everywhere present, she has not that hideous mien,

> "Which to be hated needs but to be seen,"

but is always beautiful and attractive. Ten thousand temptations assail one on every hand —temptations just suited to his character, inclination, and tastes. "Live while you live," seems to be the motto of the Parisian. The predominating characteristic of this brilliant city is thoughtless frivolity—amusement for the present, with no serious regard for the future. It must be hard to be a Christian in this great Vanity Fair. For myself, when returning from the American Chapel one Sabbath, through the Champs Elysees, surrounded by everything to divert the attention and call the mind away from serious things; with soft music wooing the ear, and gay equipages attracting the eye; with itinerant tumblers and mountebanks of every description; with Punch and Judy shows, before which crowds of people were standing in high glee; with fountains flashing in the sunlight, and fairy boats, and elevators, and hobby-horses in ceaseless motion; with vast throngs of the gay, the lively, and the beautiful, sitting, or walking, or riding; with all the life, bustle and vivacity of the French people around me, I found it necessary again and again to say, as I passed along, "Remember that you have an immortal soul to save."

And this was on the Sabbath! And such would foreign infidels make our Sabbaths, if possible. God grant that America may never witness such a fearful defiance of Him who has bidden us remember His sacred day of rest to keep it holy.

And this is Paris, where Vice is under governmental patronage, and Virtue too often is but a name! where vice is made attractive, and the stern virtues of the Christian life seem austere and repulsive. And is this the city in which it is safe for our American citizens to leave their sons, with ample means of dissipation?

During a visit to Europe, one usually finds his interest enlisted by the antiquity of the objects which he sees around. Age is novelty, and things are new to him because they are old. But the Bois de Boulogne is an exception to this. It is a splendid park just outside the city, which has been completed within three years. Napoleon found it a wilderness, the resort of duellists and suicides, and has left it a garden. Its fountains, and lakes, and cascades; its grottoes, formed of stone brought from a distance, but which seem to have grown together for ages; its race-courses, and drives, and promenades; its romantic dells and fairy bridges; its tasteful lawns, and hills, and valleys—all alive with people who have come out to breathe the pure air—are a monument of the genius and will of the Emperor. He did not wait for trees to grow, but transplanted them hither full-grown. With his admirable apparatus, summer and winter were alike, and the trees kept on growing in their new soil as if nothing had happened.

Returning from this noble park, and pausing a moment at the Chapel of St. Ferdinand to see a fine painting of the death of the Duke of Orleans, we cross the Seine in front of the Legislative buildings, and, passing through the Champ de Mars, visit the Chapel of the Invalids, where the remains of Napoleon I. now find rest. Still farther eastward, we enter the famous Jardin des Plantes, or the Botanical Garden of Paris. It is a spot well worth a long visit. There you may find almost every variety of tree, from the American pine to the Asiatic palm, all in as good condition as if in their native soil. Countless varieties of plants are here, and animals innumerable. And all this collection is maintained by the State, at a vast expense, and is free alike to the poor and the rich of Paris. Truly, the Emperor has a way of doing things which is not like ours. Think of the popular instruction, and the impetus given to popular inquiry and education by means of this open Garden of Plants. True, the money to support it comes from the people in the shape of heavy taxes, but it returns to them again, in the shape of instruction and amusement; while our money comes from us in the same way, and returns to—the pockets of our officials!

Passing still onward beyond the city limits, we come to Pere la Chaise, the great cemetery of Paris. It has no attractions, except the names of those who are buried there. Here is the tomb of Abelard and Heloise, with whose history all are familiar; here, too, lie Talma and Rachel, and other celebrities of Paris and of France.

Returning, we pass the column of July, erected upon the very spot where once stood that hated Bastile, which was destroyed in 1789, and the key of which was sent to our Washington by Lafayette. This key may still be seen at Mount Vernon. Prisoners in the Bastile were consigned to a living death. Revenge was gratified by their incarceration, and tyranny soon forgot its victim, who lingered on hopelessly, till death relieved the captive. I remember reading, when quite young, the story of a man imprisoned in the Bastile for many years, who, when he was released, found that his dwelling had been long replaced by others, his family scattered or deceased, and himself homeless and without a friend. So he returned to his prison, and begged to be admitted once more to his lonely dungeon, which he had been so happy to leave a few hours before. Here fell the Archbishop of Paris while attempting to reason with the insurgents of 1848. His last words were, "May my blood be the last spilt in civil war." Passing homeward, let us take in our way the manufactory of Gobelin tapestry. These splendid tapestries equal, in their superb finish, the very best paintings, and are woven with many hundred different shades of color. The manufactory was founded, it is said, by a man named Gobelin, a dyer, and is now monopolized by the government. The products of it are given as presents to the nobility and to the crowned heads of Europe, Queen Victoria, for instance, having several of them in her palaces. Portraits are sometimes copied in this way, as those of the Emperor and the Empress —who is a very beautiful woman—which are now being wrought from a picture by one of the finest artists of France.

Let us now return from this general survey of the city, to look at some of its churches.

Just a moment's walk from our hotel, in the Rue St. Honore, stands the church of St. Roch, begun in 1653, by Louis XIV. You enter it through two ranges of Doric and Corinthian columns, which make a front of 84 feet broad by 91 high, and find a splendid building 405 feet long. Near the entrance is the tomb of Pierre Corneille. Along the side of the church are eight or ten chapels, richly decorated with paintings, frescoes and statuary. Standing near one of the vast columns is the pulpit, formed of statues of the Evangelists, carved in oak, while a gilt angel, with outspread wings, supports the canopy. Passing behind the choir, we come to a shrine made of the cedar of Lebanon, richly decorated with mouldings of gold and bronze. Still beyond this is the chapel of the holy Sacrament,—magnificently furnished to represent the Holy of Holies,—built of rich marble, and containing all the ornaments of the Jewish ritual; re-producing, as far as art and genius and wealth can do it, the splendid scenery of the Temple at Jerusalem. In the choir stands a fine-toned organ, which, on festival occasions, alternates with a still finer and more magnificent one that is placed over the main entrance. The music in this church is said to be the best in Paris; it is certainly of the most artistic character. A service here is a novelty to an American. The number of priests who engage in it, the richness of their garments, the character of the music, the appearance of the beadles as they walk up and down the marble aisles, bringing their heavy staves of office down upon the floor with a sound that makes one start and wonder what is coming next; the women collecting their sous for the use of the chairs and *prie-dieux;* the priests passing among the crowd, during the service, to gather money for the church; the hum of voices in the chapel while service is progressing in the choir; the clouds of incense that are ascending at the altar; the splendid works of art that shine out from the ceiling, the walls and every angle of the vast edifice,—combine to make the whole a scene not soon to be forgotten.

But let us pass from this to the church of the Madeleine,—the pride of Paris, and one of the noblest specimens of modern genius and art that the world contains. Although begun in 1704, it was not finished until the time of Louis Phillippe. It cost 13,079,000 francs. Its architecture is Grecian, being surrounded by 52 Corinthian columns, 49 feet high and $16\frac{1}{2}$ feet in circumference. In the walls are 32 niches filled with statues of saints. Before you ascend the lofty flight of 28 steps, you notice that the whole entablature and ceiling are profusely decorated with the most elaborate sculpture. Look also to the pediment of the southern front, where is an immense alto-relievo, 126 feet by 24. In the centre is the figure of Christ, with Magdalen at His feet; to His right, the angels of mercy, Innocence and Faith. In the corner, an angel is greeting a spirit just rising to bliss; and on the left of the Sovereign Judge the angel of vengeance is repelling hatred, unchastity, hypocrisy and avarice, while a demon is precipitating to the abyss a lost and damned spirit.

Ascending the steps, pause, and study the magnificent bronze doors,—outvying all but those of St. Peter's, at Rome, measuring 33 by $16\frac{1}{2}$ feet, and displaying in bas-relief Scriptural illustrations of the Decalogue, leaving out the second, and dividing the tenth Commandment.

As you enter, you are amazed at the magnificence and artistic beauty that meet you. Over the porch stands a superb Corinthian organ. On the right is the chapel for marriages, with a group representing the marriage of the Virgin. On the left, the Baptismal font, with a representation of the Baptism of Christ at Jordan. There are twelve confessionals, with a pulpit richly carved in oak, and gilt, and decorated like the organ. The church consists of one vast nave, interrupted by piers, fronted with lofty columns, supporting colossal arches, on which rest three cupolas with skylights spendidly decorated, and supported in the corners by figures of the Apostles. The richest marbles encrust the walls of the church. The floor also is of rich and variegated marble. The walls of the choir are ornamented with paintings and arabesques on a ground of *gold*. The ceilings are decorated with magnificent frescoes, representing the propagation of Christianity.

In the midst of the church, above a flight of marble steps, stands the high altar, surrounded by a group of statuary, among which the principal figure is Magdalen, borne upwards on the wings of angels. At each corner on a pedestal stands an archangel in prayer.

For these figures, alone, 150,000 francs were paid!

While sitting in this church I took out my Testament and turned to the Epistle to the Hebrews, where Christ is spoken of as our only great High Priest; and thought how it set aside all this pomp and pageant as utterly useless in the worship of the Christian Church; and felt that when the word of God should come to be an open volume in France, as it is in Scotland, these splendid services would be replaced by a purer, and simpler, and more spiritual worship, in harmony with the order of God's house, and better adapted to lead the soul to Christ, and salvation.

III.

THE CHURCHES AND PALACES OF PARIS.

WE will take a brief glance at two or three more of the churches of Paris, and then enter some of its most celebraced Palaces and Museums. First in reputation, if not in beauty, is the cathedral of Notre Dame. It stands upon an island called *la Cité*, near the spot where once stood a Roman temple—an altar of which was discovered in the year 1711. It is supposed that as early as A. D. 365 a church was built here, which was afterwards enlarged by Childebert. The foundations of Notre Dame were laid A. D. 1000, and in 1185, the Patriarch of Jerusalem, who had visited Paris to preach up the first Crusade, officiated in the church. Age after age witnessed some addition to the noble pile, which now presents a fine specimen of the Gothic architecture of the 12th century. The cathedral is 390 feet long, 144 feet in width, and 142 feet high. Three vast arched portals lead to the interior from the front. Over these are circular windows 36 feet in diameter. As you enter the middle door-way, you see an elaborate representation in bas-relief of the Judgment. The angels are sounding the last trumpet—the dead are rising—the separation of the righteous and the wicked is taking place—and the Saviour is upon the throne, surrounded by His angels and the emblems of His passion. On the sides of the portal are 24 figures representing 12 virtues and their opposite vices. Beyond these are four other bas-reliefs: the offering of Isaac—the departure of Abraham—Job witnessing the destruction of his flocks—and Job reproving his wife. On the massive doors are carved Christ bearing His Cross, and the Virgin in her sorrow. Apostles, patriarchs and kings fill up the niches which are left on either hand. The other two entrances resemble this in their elaborate designs, only differing in the scenes represented. Above these is a gallery of small pillars containing statues of some of the French sovereigns. Looking still higher up you see a colossal statue of the Virgin, between two angels, and on either side a figure of Adam and Eve. Over this is a vast central window, and above all rises a lofty gallery of slender shafts, while on either corner is a noble tower 204 feet in height.

Passing round to the south side of the church, we come to another arched entrance, ornamented with bas-reliefs of scenes in the life of Stephen. In the rear are innumerable columns, buttresses, figures, and shafts, at whose elaborate designs one gazes with wonder. The north side also has an entrance on which are figures and statues representing the Virgin crushing the Dragon—the Nativity, and the Adoration of the Magi. The Porte-Rouge is another splendid portal, between which and the eastern angle of the church are carvings which represent the Death, Funeral, and Assumption of the Virgin—Christ with the Angels, and Christ with the Virgin on a throne, the Virgin in an agony at the feet of the Saviour, and also delivering a woman who is about to sell herself to the Devil. Such is a general view of the exterior of the noble edifice. Within we find a vast series of columns, chapels, arches, pictures, altars, and statues, which would require many weeks to study and comprehend, and to which no description can do full justice.

In this cathedral are performed the State ceremonies of France. Here the first Napoleon was crowned Emperor; here the present Emperor was married, and here, when the people shall call for the ceremony, the Third Napoleon will be crowned—for although the Emperor, he has not yet received the crown of France.

On the occasion of the solemn *Te Deum* for the success of the French arms at Magenta, the soldiers of the National Guard and of the regular army were drawn up on either side, from the Tuileries to the cathedral, and these lines were themselves a magnificent sight.

The scene which I had the pleasure of witnessing was thus described in *Galignani's Messenger:*

"The cortege left the Tuileries by the Carrousel, and then followed the Rue de Rivoli. A squadron of the mounted municipal guard headed the cortege, after whom came the carriages of the Princess Mathilde, the Princess Clotilda, and next that of the Empress, who was accompanied by Prince Jerome. Her Majesty wore a violet silk dress, a chapeau of white crape, ornamented with a violet feather, and a white lace shawl. Marshal Magnan and General the Marquis de Lawœstine, followed by a numerous staff, escorted the Imperial carriage, which was followed by detachments of lancers of the Imperial Guard and of the 6th Dragoons. The preparations made at the cathedral were on a grand scale. In the middle of the choir, opposite the altar, was placed a chair of state for the Empress Regent, with seats for Prince Jerome, the Princess Clotilda, the Princess Mathilde, and the other princes and princesses of the Imperial family. Places were also arranged for the cardinals, bishops, marshals, admirals, grand officers of the Crown, the household of the Empress, members of the

Senate, Legislative Body, and Council of State, as well as accommodation for different constituted bodies. A second salute announced the close of the ceremony, when her Majesty and the cortege returned to the Tuileries in the same state in which they had left it. A violent storm of thunder, lightning and heavy rain burst over Paris just as the Empress arrived at the cathedral, and had ceased before the ceremony had concluded. At night, the public offices, theatres, and a vast number of private houses, were again most brilliantly illuminated."

In the sacristy of the cathedral is a museum of religious curiosities and relics, which have been collecting for ages. This church, with, indeed, all the old churches of Paris, is now undergoing thorough repairs, under the supervision of the Emperor, who seems determined to preserve them in their original beauty and splendor.

Passing away from this spot, we come to the church of St. Germain l'Auxerrois, which is over nine centuries old, and has wonderfully escaped the devastations of the Revolutionary mobs of

Paris. The exterior of the church is decorated with bas-reliefs and statues, and the interior is gorgeous beyond all power of words to describe, with frescoes and paintings, statues and columns, altars and chapels, covered with gold. But its chief interest is its historic recollections.

Early in the progress of the Reformation, the truths of the gospel began to awaken the people of France from the slumbers of spiritual death. When the Protestant Church assumed a distinct organization, its principal features were like those of the other continental churches, being distinctly and decidedly Presbyterian.

The first General Assembly was held in 1559, one year before a similar body first met in Scotland. In the course of twelve years 2150 churches had been established throughout France, some of which enrolled as many as 7,000 members, among whom were many of the noblest men of the age. The Huguenots had obtained, as they supposed, liberty of conscience and immunity from further wrong; and Charles IX., King of France, in order to lull them into security, and thus prepare the way for his bloody purpose, declared that he was convinced of the impossibility of forcing men's consciences, and that he had determined to allow every man the free exercise of his religion. The Huguenot leaders were loaded with favors, and this deception was kept up for two years, until all suspicion was completely lulled. On the occasion of the marriage of the King's daughter Margaret, with Henry of Navarre, all of the royal and noble Protestants were invited to Paris to witness this union—a new pledge of reconciliation and concession. They came, and the plot was ripe for execution. Sixty thousand armed men were collected in the city, and the curtain rose upon the dreadful and bloody drama of St. Bartholomew's Eve, the 24th of August, 1572.

A little after midnight the deep tones of the cathedral bell summoned the soldiers to their work of death. First perished the Admiral Coligny, and then, at the sound of the bell of the Palais de Justice, *the massacre of St. Bartholomew began.* At the signal, every Catholic, having been forewarned, placed a light in his window and a white cross upon his cap, bound a white scarf upon his arm, and then rushed forth to the slaughter of the heretics. The dwellings of the Protestants were attacked, and the inmates dragged forth to death. The streets ran blood; and the groans of the dying, the shrieks of the wounded, and the imploring cries of women and children, made music for the actors in this horrid drama of death. The King looked out upon the scene with frantic and fiendish joy; the ladies of the court amused themselves with looking at the dead bodies of those slain within the palace, with whom they had been engaged in social intercourse a few short hours before. Sixty thousand men hunted down their brethren. For seven days this dreadful slaughter continued, and over ten thousand Protestants perished in Paris alone, and sixty thousand more throughout France.

The news was received at Rome with excessive joy. The Cardinal Lorraine rewarded the messenger who brought the tidings of these unparalleled atrocities with a gift of ten thousand crowns. At Lyons, the Pope's legate absolved the murderers, by making over them the sign of the cross. Pope Gregory XIII. congratulated the King on the successful completion of a purpose "*so long meditated and so happily executed for the good of religion,*" and triumphal medals were struck, commemorating the occasion. Thus Rome perpetuated her shame, and gave her sanction to the massacre of thousands of innocent and unoffending Christians. This is all matter of history, and, try as he may, Bishop Hughes cannot blot out the record, though he may efface it from our schoolbooks.

When I entered this church of St. Germain I recalled these scenes of St. Bartholomew, for it was in the tower of this cathedral that the fatal signal was given for the Massacre. All night long its bells were tolling, mingling their deep vibrations with the shrieks of the wounded and the groans of the dying. As I passed down its aisles, indifferent to its gorgeous decorations—thinking only of the scenes with which it was associated—the bell struck the hour, and as its heavy tones sounded upon my ear I started from my reverie as though I were hearing again the awful summons to the work of death.

Passing away from this spot, we come to the Pantheon, built upon the ruins of St. Geneveive by Madame Pompadour,—a pretty person to build a church! The funds were raised by *lottery*. The dome of the church is 268 feet high, and the whole edifice is a noble pile of architecture. Its pillars and walls still bear the marks of the last Revolution.

We must not omit the most splendid of the churches of Paris, the Sainte Chapelle, attached to the Palais de Justice, which, in the magnificence of its statuary, frescoes, paintings and decorations, excells all the rest. The form of the church is somewhat peculiar. It is one hundred and eight feet long, fifty-five feet in breadth, and one hundred and thirty-nine feet in height— higher than it is long or broad. I will not attempt to describe this wonderful church. Among its relics is, of course, a piece of the True Cross. There are very few churches upon the Continent which are destitute of this relic.

I have no doubt that there are enough pieces of the True Cross in the different Continental churches to make several of the size of the original. I have often thought, in looking at such relics, of a visit which a gentleman paid to one of these churches, with a native of the Green Isle for a *cicerone*. "Here," said the Irishman, "is the sword with which Balaam slew the ass." "But Balaam didn't *have* any sword," replied the visitor; "he only wished for one, with which to smite the animal." "Eh?" rejoined the Irishman; "Well, then, this is the sword which Balaam wished for." Many of the relics which I saw were of a similar character.

A great contrast to all this splendor and folly is seen in the American Chapel, in the Rue de Berri. I found here a noble band of earnest and faithful Christians laboring for the good of souls. Episcopal services were held in the morning, and in the afternoon the form of worship was like our own. On both occasions Christians of all denominations united with evident cordiality and good feeling.

There was also a most promising Bible-class,

under the tuition of an American gentleman, resident in Paris.

But leaving the churches, let us take a glimpse at some of the palaces of France. Our first visit is to Versailles, which we reach by rail in half an hour. Walking up a fine old boulevard, which leads through the town, we come to the Rue de Reservoirs, which terminates at the palace. Three hundred years ago this spot was an immense forest, which had been the great hunting-ground of the Court of France. Here Louis XIII. built a pavilion in which to rest after the toils of the chase. Louis XIV. at length came to the throne, a monarch who loved pleasure and who followed it through all the fearful mazes of a guilty life, surrounding himself with every appliance which his voluptuous nature demanded. His palace stood near the church of St. Denis, where lay the bones of his ancestors, and he could not bear the proximity of these silent monitors. The nearness of the tomb, and its stern and awful realities, interfered with his life of guilty pleasure, and brought thoughts of death—thoughts which he hated most—to his mind. He wished to live undisturbed by such gloomy reflections, and as it was the custom then, he believed that the common people lived solely for their monarch's pleasure, and accumulated wealth only that their masters might spend it, and determined to build Versailles, at a distance from St. Denis and its melancholy thoughts. Upon this palace he lavished the immense sum of $200,000,000, and in its erection 30,000 soldiers, besides mechanics and laborers innumerable, were employed, and the place soon contained a population of one hundred thousand persons. The surrounding wilderness became a garden surpassing all description, filled with statues, groves, fountains, lawns, and wonders of nature and of art, rivalling Babylon in beauty and grandeur. Words fail to describe this royal abode; no pencil can do it justice, and even sight itself fails, amid so many dazzling scenes.

The palace is built with a projecting centre, and two extensive wings, and contains over five hundred rooms, filled with paintings and statues. The front of the building is about twelve hundred feet long, and one travels nearly a quarter of a mile in going from one end to the other of this immense pile. On the extreme right wing, occupying about as much space in comparison with the rest of the building as does a little bed-room over the stairs, or a closet, in an ordinary house, is a splendid theatre, in which sat the beauties of the Courts of Louis XIV. and XV. and of the kings since their reigns, to witness the performances of the best actors of the age.

Pause for a moment in the box where royalty once sat, with all the frail beauties of the French court, and recall the past. Think how the lost and infamous, though beautiful creatures of the French kings trod these halls even in the presence of the queens whom they had displaced from their monarch's affections. Recall the misery and woe under which many a noble heart here sank down with sorrow, and learn a sad but impressive lesson of the terrible results of sin, and the fearful examples of splendid misery which the history of France presents.

Upon that stage poor Marie Antoinette once

sank down with shame and grief while enacting a tragedy (too soon to be followed by one far more terrible), when she heard the hiss of her dissolute husband. There operas were performed at a nightly expense of $25,000, paid for by the poor toiling millions of France, and there the excited and angry mob held its revels when it had broken down the power of royalty, and hung the inmates of the surrounding palaces at their very gates.

Passing out of this place with its terrible memories, we enter a vast gallery of sculpture of the kings and queens of France. Parallel to this are two other halls of equal length, (300 feet,) the one devoted to paintings descriptive of French history, and the other to the story of Constantine, &c.

Leaving these halls, we enter the Royal Chapel, gorgeously fitted up, to which the dissolute Court used to retire to atone for days of sin by an hour of worship; and feeling a sentiment of awe at the surroundings of religion, imagined themselves forgiven, and went out to new sin. Religion was fashionable then, and went in silver slippers, and they evidently thought that they had solved the problem, how sin and piety could exist together. Crowds went to church more to see the king than to worship. To test this, a maitre one day announced that the king would not be present at chapel that day, and in a few moments the church was empty.

Here, at yonder magnificent altar, Marie Antoinette was married, and began that sad drama which was at length terminated amid the horrors of the guillotine, and the taunts and execrations of the cruel mob that was thirsting for her blood. Passing hence through the Saloon of Hercules, and other halls named after mythological characters, and fitted up to correspond with the name, the eye is dazzled with their varied beauties. The ceilings are adorned with the finest frescoes, and rich, gilded cornices; while splendid paintings, and furniture of the most costly kind, meet you at every turn. Here is the Looking-Glass Gallery, 242 feet long, by 35 wide, and 42 feet high. Turning to the left, we come to the private rooms of the royal family.

Here is the cabinet of Louis XIV., into which Madame du Barry, one of his courtesans, once entered, while the king was busy, snatched a bundle of State papers from his hand and threw them into the fire, the king laughing gaily the while. That same du Barry, a short time afterwards, called out, while in the grasp of a rude mob, for "Life!" "life!" while the only replies to her entreaties were brutal jests upon the soft pillow which the guillotine would make for that fair head. Surrounded by a drunken and maddened mob, she was dragged in a cart to the block. Her long tresses, with which the king had often dallied, were shorn from her head, and from the struggling victim was heard the piteous cry of "Save me, save me!" But her distress and her dangerous beauty only drew upon her the rude laugh of the rabble. With coarse violence her executioners bound her to the fatal plank; the glittering knife fell, and her limbs relaxed in death as her head fell into the trough—and all was over. Hurrying away from these apartments, we enter the small rooms of the king.

Here is the luxurious bed-chamber, in which Louis XIV. died—for even kings must die—upon a splendid couch, decorated as one would imagine the bed of so profligate a monarch to be, attended only by an old and withered woman, for all his Court had fled and left him alone with that loathsome disease, the small-pox. The furniture of this bed-room was twelve years in making.

Here, too, died Louis XV., surrounded by his courtiers, to whom he said, with a most touching pathos, "Gentlemen, gentlemen, I implore your pardon for the bad example I have set you. Think of me sometimes, I pray you! O God, come to my aid and help me." Fit commentary upon his career. A vast throng stood in the court-yard awaiting the tidings of his death. An officer of the household took a staff and broke it, saying, "Gentlemen, the king is dead," and then raising another rod, shouted, "*Vive le Roi*," and the throng welcomed the rising Star of France, and forgot him whose light was quenched in the night of the grave.

Passing onward through splendid suites of

rooms, we come to the queen's bed-chamber Here it was that Marie Antoinette sought for rest and shelter when the mob was thundering at the gates of the palace. From this spot she escaped with her life, only to fall by a more fearful death after her trial before the Revolutionary tribunal.

But we cannot linger here. Gallery succeeds to gallery in this wonderful spot, each one vying with the other in interest and beauty—or being a repetition of previous splendors. Everywhere we meet some new monument of taste, wealth, beauty, and folly. We might pause here for days, for there are hundreds of rooms, and thousands of pictures, and jewels, and statues, and objects of historic interest. Here is the spot where Madame Montespan, who had left her husband to become the mother of the children of an abandoned king, when ordered to leave the palace, seized a knife and attempted to take the life of her child. Here lived Madame Maintenon, who succeeded in the short-lived affections of the monarch. Here flourished the most majestic of all the Bourbons, of whom it was said, "They who occupy thrones are the most unfortunate in the world."

Going out of the palace, one notices statues in every angle, chief among which is the equestrian statue of Louis XIV. The State carriages also attract attention, that of Charles X. costing $100,000, as much money as our President receives for his four years' services.

The Park of Versailles is immense, containing about thirty-two thousand acres, and is dotted here and there with small palaces, among which is the Petite Trianon, splendidly furnished and built in the Roman style, and in which the king used to retire and play the part of an humble innkeeper, the ladies and gentlemen of his court acting in various capacities—one as the baker, another as the cook, and so on, forgetting for a while their rank, and occupying themselves with the cares of humble life. This palace was built for Madame du Barry, but has been successively occupied by all the queens of France; and here lived the first Napoleon with his Josephine.

There is one solemn lesson to be drawn from

this scene—the vanity of human greatness and glory. It was short pleasure and long woe. Far better piety, even in poverty and sorrow, than to march, in royal robes and gilded crowns, to eternal misery and death. God grant that we may never see such sights here, but that Americans, satisfied with their quiet homes—the abodes of love, peace, virtue, and purity—may continue to live in Republican simplicity, and refuse to imitate either the vices or the splendor of European courts.

IV.

PARIS TO LYONS.

WE have time to take but a parting glance at two or three more of the objects of interest in Paris.—To begin with the Tuileries, the present residence of the Emperor. The palace is about 1,000 feet long, by 118 wide. We pass up a broad staircase, and through suites of rooms, galleries, and saloons, in some respects surpassing in richness and splendor those of Versailles. Draperies of velvet and gold, richly frescoed ceilings, exquisite paintings, statues of marble, bronze, and silver, and carpets woven in the looms of the Gobelins, make up the sights which are to be seen here. The hangings of the Throne Room are of dark red velvet, manufactured at Lyons, with palm leaves and wreaths wrought in gold. The throne is canopied with the same material, and stands upon an elevated platform, upon the back of which is the imperial eagle, surrounded by a wreath of gold.

But we cannot pause here, except to look out from the large centre window and admire the magnificent scene which stretches before us, and to think of the sad fate of many who once lived amid these splendors, and who, during the Revolutions of France, passed away like a dream.

Here dwelt the First Consul, and when he was declared Emperor, it was again his home. Here dwelt the royal family after the restoration, until the palace was again attacked by the mob of 1830. Here lived Louis Phillippe, when he was recalled to his throne by the cries of *Vive le Roi!* and here he signed his abdication, when the garden of the Tuileries was filled with a fierce and angry mob, from which he barely escaped with his life. And here lives the present Napoleon; but for how long who can predict? It may be for life; it may be that the next steamer may bring the news of his abdication, or of his death. Alas! France wants the elements of a stable government. She needs what it will take ages to give her: the Family, Home, the Bible, and the Sabbath. Perpetual life out of doors; the confusion of the first day of the week, with all the others; and a religion given by priests, are enough to make any government unstable.

Leaving the Tuileries, we enter the ancient palace of the Louvre, with its vast halls and saloons filled with rich collections of paintings and sculptures, and historical and antique curiosities. It is the work of a day simple to pass through it. Here is the Antique Museum, made up of statues, bas-reliefs, and frescoes, from Egypt, Greece, and Rome, which seem to have reproduced the arts of these countries and fixed them in all their varied extent and beauty.

The Museum of the Sovereigns is composed of the relics of the kings and queens of France. Here is the shoe of Marie Antoinette; the sceptre of Charlemagne; the crown of Louis XVI.; and the writing-desk of Louis Phillippe. But we pause longest, and with most indescribable feelings, in the room wholly devoted to the articles owned and used by Napoleon I. Here is his full dress, worn on State occasions; his saddle; his gloves; his uniform, worn at Marengo; the hat he wore at St. Helena, and the handkerchief with which the death-damps were wiped from his brow when he passed away forever from the dreams of battle.

But, giving a rapid glance at the Marine Museum, filled with models of the ships, seaports, and public docks of France; at the Assyrian Gallery, at the Museum of Modern Sculpture, Paintings, &c., we must hasten to the Luxembourg, a palace which was built for Marie de Médicis, in 1612, where we find a repetition of the magnificence of the Tuileries and the galleries of the Louvre. Leaving this, we visit the Hotel de Cluny, one of the finest remaining specimens of the ancient mansions of the sixteenth century. It was built about the year 1480, upon the ruins of an ancient Roman bath, and was inhabited by Mary, the sister of Henry VIII., of England, and the widow of Louis XII., of France. After passing through many hands, it is now in possession of the government, which has restored it to its former appearance, so that it presents an exact fac simile of a Parisian mansion in the sixteenth century. Even in the furnishing of the rooms, this idea is carried out, and they are crowded with relics of an intensely interesting historical character. Here we find beautiful tapestry, ecclesiastical dresses of almost every age, curious suits of armor, old furniture, crockery, enamels, glass ware, antique beds, quaint ear-rings, altar-pieces, and, in short, everything necessary to give a correct idea of life in the earlier ages of the French nation. Near this museum are the remains of an ancient Roman palace, in which Julian lived when he was declared Emperor by his troops.

But leaving unnoticed many scenes of great interest, we hasten to our hotel, and bidding adieu to our hostess, and to Paris, we take tickets for Fontainebleau, on our way to Lyons.

For my part, I quitted the city without a regret. I had spent two weeks there looking at its wonders, and recalling the thrilling histories which are connected with its monuments; but I had little sympathy with that gay, excitable, and pleasure-loving people. If I had no soul to save, or God to serve, I might be content to live there. But I sat down in the car—saw the conductor lock the door—heard the shriek of the locomotive; saw the train move on; knew that I was probably never to see that beautiful city again, and was whirled away into the valley of the Seine without a sigh of regret for all that I was leaving behind me. God forbid that our own land should ever number among its cities one like Paris—great, powerful, and magnificent as it is.

For many miles it is visible, as we pass on southward, through smiling fields and picturesque villages, skirting the bright waters of the Seine. It is the season of harvest, and the fields are alive with the peasantry—young and old, men, women, and children—busily engaged in reaping the golden grain or gathering it into bundles. A ride of forty miles brings us to the station of Fontainebleau, which we reach over a splendid viaduct of thirty arches. This is a city of about 10,000 inhabitants, but with few attractions, save the splendid palace, which stands upon the outskirts of a vast forest, the famous hunting-ground of the kings of France, the scene of exciting dramas and magnificent displays upon which the curtain of death has now fallen. Three hundred years ago the present chateau was built. Here were held princely revels when Charles of Germany was the guest of Francis. Here was signed the revocation of the Edict of Nantes, so fatal to the Protestant cause in France. Here Napoleon announced to Josephine his intended divorce; and here, standing upon those stairs, he reviewed his army and took leave of it, when he had signed his abdication.

I need not attempt a description of Fontainebleau. It is but a repetition of Versailles, with its memorials of regal grandeur, and its sad and touching lessons of the transitory and uncertain nature of all earthly glory. You wander through vast saloons and galleries filled with the wealth of ages, and think of Marie Antoinette and her tragic end; and Josephine, with her painful and sad story; and Napoleon, whose star went down amid storm and darkness. You wander over the splendid gardens and grounds, recall the time when they witnessed the mustering of gay courtiers and dashing huntsmen, and heard the call of the bugle and the deep baying of the hounds. You think of the times when the vast avenues were crowded with the equipages of princes, who swept upwards towards these festal halls, now all deserted and silent, save when curious visitors enter them, and hurry through, little heeding the sad stories they might tell.

All has vanished of this splendor. The pageant has gone by. Glad voices are hushed. Bright eyes are quenched in death. The robe and the sceptre and the diadem are exchanged for the cerements of the grave.

Entering the cars again, we are whirled through a beautiful and fertile country, and by many a fine and populous city, until we reach Lyons and the Hotel Callet.

A letter of introduction to our consul, Hon. J. W. White, procured for us the kind attentions of himself and family. It affords me great pleasure thus publicly to speak of our representative in that city, one who well sustains the reputation of America, and who by his official and private character has secured the respect and esteem of the citizens of Lyons, and the grateful memory of many who have received his attentions and kindness.

I met at his house the venerable Count de Castellane, the oldest Marshal of France, who was an officer under the first Napoleon during the Russian campaign. At his advanced age he is still hale and hearty, and has the charge of one hundred thousand soldiers.

The city of Lyons has a population of about 275,000 inhabitants, and is built on a tongue of land, about three miles long, between the rivers Seine and Rhone, the one having swept down hither from the northern slope of the Jura mountains, the other from the tremendous glaciers of Switzerland, through the pure waters of Lake Leman. Wending our way to the citadel, commanding the town, from which we have a magnificent view of the valley of the Rhone; we can see the vast ranges of hills, terminating in the Alps, prominent among which is the glittering summit of Mont Blanc. In the rear of this terrace is the cathedral of Notre Dame, on whose tower is a statue of the Virgin, twenty-eight feet high. Not far from this is the old church of St. Irenæus, built over an ancient crypt used by the early Christians of Lyons. An old woman, intensely French, bearing a lighted candle, preceded us down into the crypt. Calling our attention to the ancient pavement, which remains unaltered since it was first laid, she leads the way to the tombs of Irenæus and other early Christians; and also to the tomb of a female, who, in her misapplied devotion, spent the closing years of her life, which she should have adorned by deeds of active charity, in this subterranean abode, counting over her beads, saying her prayers, and thinking that she was serving God. Still farther on is a grated window, looking into a dark vault, where are collected the bones of nineteen thousand martyrs, who are said to have perished in the first ages of the church.

In the fine Gothic cathedral of St. Jean, begun in the seventh century, we witnessed the ceremonies of the grand Te Deum, in honor of the victory of Magenta. Climbing up, through suffocating staircases, into a gallery sixty feet from the floor, we had a full view of the magnificent procession, composed of officers of rank, cardinals, priests, acolytes, and soldiers, as it entered the church. The soldiers went through their drill at the word of command and at the tap of the drum, while the religious services went on, in no wise interrupted by the crash of arms.

One of the most interesting features of Lyons is her manufactories of silk. In the high parts of the city, amid old houses and steep and narrow streets, we find a large portion of the suburbs devoted to this business. There are about 32,000 looms engaged in it. These factories are not large, like our cotton mills, but a proprietor rents out an ordinary house to a factor, who fills it with looms. Frequently the work-shop and dwelling apartments are in the same house, so that the operations are most economical. They have carried their work to great perfection, being able to weave into the silk the most exquisite pictures and portraits. The machinery for the work resembles, in its general details, the power carpet-looms. There are 38,000 men employed at this work, and their influence in the city sometimes makes the greatest police vigilance necessary, especially in times of panic and commercial depression. During the last crisis, when hundreds were out of employment and clamoring for bread, the Emperor ordered the Bois de Boulogne, a large park, to be laid out, and so furnished employment for fourteen hundred men, saving as many families from want, and making himself intensely popular.

Lyons, although a Roman Catholic city, has several Protestant churches, which are sources of great good to the people. I attended service at the English Episcopal chapel, where I heard a most excellent sermon from Mr. Barter, who also administered the Sacrament of the Lord's Supper. As I partook of these consecrated elements in that city, far away from home, I felt that I could heartily join in repeating the creed and saying, "I believe in the communion of saints!"

I attended also the French chapel, under the Rev. Mr. Cordes, whose acquaintance I made, and from whom I learned many interesting facts in regard to the work which is going on in the south of France. Here is a most hopeful field for effort, for in the French Catholics there is a substratum of genuine piety which makes them peculiarly susceptible to evangelical truths. The Protestant Church here is *Presbyterian*. Part of it is supported by government, and thus is obliged to submit to governmental interference. In consequence of evils that have thus arisen, especially in regard to proper church discipline, a new church has been formed, independent of the State, and is supported by many faithful and pious men, and they are doing a great and good work. Even among Catholics, they find most hopeful cases of conversion. Among the instances related to me, was that of a poor woman who became convicted of sin. She went to her priest, and he advised her to make a nine days' pilgrimage to the church of St. Fouvrière, dedicated to Mary. She attended to his counsel, but found no relief. The burden was still upon her heart. The priest gave her some pictures, and told her to study them and repeat so many prayers. This she did faithfully, but with no better result. Then the priest gave her some images to look at and pray, and assured her she would find peace. She followed his advice, but no peace came. At length she became ill and took to her bed. Here a Protestant sister found her, and learned the cause of her sickness. She told her she had a remedy. She took the Scriptures and read to her the words of Jesus and His precious promises. Peace came to her heart—she recovered her health, and lived and died a sincere believer in Christ. There is a great deal of interest manifested in Sabbath-schools, and much is doing for the instruction of children. They have also Bible-classes for adults, and there are Bible-readers who go from house to house, among the poor, opening to them the Scriptures, and teaching them the way of salvation. The work of the Protestant church lies chiefly among the poor and the middle classes, as the aristocracy or nobility are Catholics.

But I was happy to hear that the Emperor, while himself a rigid papist, is desirous to have full religious liberty in France. And a case was related where he had interfered to set at liberty four persons who were victims of priestly intolerance, and had been put in prison for preaching the Gospel. There are a number of Presbyterian churches in and about Lyons, and in France they have enough to form several Presbyteries and a Synod.

Many earnest inquiries were made in regard to the revival in America, and a deep interest was manifested in its progress. When I turned from Lyons, I felt that there were in operation in that city means which, with the blessing of God upon them, would accomplish immeasurable good for France.

V.

LYONS TO NAPLES.

IT was a pleasant day, in the middle of June, that we took the cars at Lyons for Montalimar, where we were to spend the night.

The road leads through a country of much interest and beauty, its fields highly cultivated, and its towns and villages exceedingly picturesque, many of them presenting abundant evidences of their high antiquity, and their Roman origin. The waters of the Rhone are flashing by us on their way to the sea, and the valley through which we are passing presents a succession of beauties, rarely surpassed. At times the river sweeps round the base of some majestic cliff, crowned with the venerable ruins of an ancient fortress, built in the era of Roman greatness and power, and then opens into a broad and lovely plain, smiling amid the glories of the harvest. Occasionally the distant and snow-clad Alps tower over the intervening hills and stand out in solemn grandeur against the soft blue sky, and its rich drapery of clouds reflects the golden beams of the setting sun.

Just at evening the train stops at the old city of Montalimar, surrounded by ramparts, abounding in queer and quaint old ruins, and chiefly devoted to the manufacture of morocco and soap! A diminutive omnibus, with a jolly fat driver, conveys us through ancient, odd-looking streets, with an indescribable appearance of having once seen better days, into the court of an old French inn, full of diligences, donkeys and fleas—especially fleas, and exceedingly active ones at that. A long and dingy-looking building, with flights of stone steps leading to interminable corridors and halls, is the Post-Inn where we are to spend the evening. Our lodging room, with its fixtures, its elaborate wainscotting, and its venerable furniture, is a curiosity, and the whole establishment presents us with a very good idea of a French inn of the olden time. The scenery around Montalimar is most brilliant and exceedingly picturesque, while the appearance of the town itself cannot fail to delight the lover of the antique.

Passing down from this city, through ever-varying beauties and splendors,—now skirting the waters of the Rhone, or crossing one of its numerous tributaries; then plunging through dark tunnels, built under large cliffs or headlands; now coming in sight of the ruins of an ancient Roman triumphal arch, or citadel, or aqueduct, or palace,—we at last pause for a while to look at the magnificent building, standing in full view at the station at Avignon, and interesting as being the ancient residence of the Pope during the schism between the churches of France and Italy, when two Popes claimed the Keys. The succession has never yet been settled, at least to our satisfaction, and we shall remain a Presbyterian until this nice point has been satisfactorily adjusted. Here Petrarch once lived and saw his Laura, whose fate was mingled so tenderly and touchingly with his own.

From Avignon our way is still southward, through a country the character of whose scenery now changes to a rugged and sublime grandeur and wildness. We turn out of our way to visit, at Nismes, a noble amphitheatre—the ruins of the Temple of Diana, and gardens and fountain, which are fine evidences of ancient art and taste. As we pass onward, we observe many women in the quaint costumes of the south of France, which would be regarded here as great curiosities. Their head-dresses are immense, rising tier upon tier—but they have very pretty faces under them, nevertheless. From Arles, a city renowned for its Roman ruins, its quaint costumes, and its beautiful women, we pass over a vast unbroken plain, which, with its marshes and lagoons, is said to resemble Africa. Hurrying by long series of ruins, tunnels, embankments, viaducts and bridges, we at length enter the suburbs of Marseilles, and just at dusk are whirled past beautiful country seats, looking out upon lofty hills, crowned with chateaux and citadels, until we stop at the station in the city. After the ordinary detention we are permitted to go to the *Hôtel des Empereurs*, to experience there a system of extortion so thorough that it would do credit to any city in Italy. We mention the name of this hotel, so that if any of our friends ever visit Marseilles they may avoid it and go to some other, to be fleeced, probably, just as badly.

Marseilles has a population of about two hundred thousand. It is beautifully situated upon, and surrounded by, hills which form a noble landmark to the sailor upon the Mediterranean. It has a fine harbor. As I sat upon the deck of the steamer, and watched the process of getting under way, and saw our ship shooting out from the midst of a fleet of vessels of all sizes and descriptions, I found sincere pleasure in looking out upon the scenes which were opening before me. Our ship was crowded with officers, soldiers, and priests, on their way to the seat of war, and we met two ships bound for France and loaded with Austrian prisoners. The coast, as we sail towards Italy, presents a variety of scenes of exceeding beauty. Four days from Marseilles, most of which time had been spent at Genoa, Leghorn and Civita Vecchia, we sighted the headlands of the Bay of Naples, and as I came upon deck and caught my first glimpse of the scene, I felt that description was surpassed, and that the half of its glories had not been told. The beautiful indentation of the shore which forms the Bay of Naples commences, on the North, at the Cape of Miseno, and sweeping round, in a most graceful curve, towards the east and south, terminates at the Capo Della Campanella, making a circuit of thirty-five miles.

As our ship rounds the northern headland, there come rapidly into view beautiful and bold shores, covered with Italian villas, palaces, gardens and convents—until the whole of this magnificent bay bursts upon the view and presents a scene which has, perhaps, no equal, and which no pen can fully describe. Almost in the centre of this glorious picture, Vesuvius, its head wreathed by the dark clouds of smoke which ceaselessly roll up from its crater, rises majestically from a lovely valley. As the eye sweeps around the beautiful coast, it takes in a series of villages and hamlets, peeping out from groves of orange, citron and olive-trees, while behind them the distant hills rise in graceful outlines, and mountains, softened by distance and mellowed by the indescribable glow of an Italian atmosphere, shut in the lovely scene.

Turning from this picture, to which words do no justice, we catch our first view of the city of Naples, which lies upon a smaller indentation of the bay. Dashing by lines of forts and castles, through fleets of small vessels, with the peculiar oriental model of the Mediterranean, which are lying quietly at anchor,—just as the morning bugle is arousing the soldiers of the castle, and the guns of the ships-of-war are thundering over the waters, we come to anchor under the range of one of the batteries, and opposite the Customhouse of Naples. During the long hours we spend in waiting for the return of our passports, which have been sent on shore to the police, we amuse ourselves by watching the small boats which surround the ship, filled with fruit or other edibles, or laden with musicians who have all the airs of opera singers, and who have come out to pick up a few pence for their performances. At last the officers of the Government are satisfied, and we are permitted to debark. Small boats now swarm about the vessel like leeches, and the boatmen tender their services most pertinaciously.

While we are wondering how we shall make our way to the shore, we hear a voice asking in good English, "Is there any one here for the *Hotel des Etrangers?*" "Yes," we replied, "It is the very hotel to which we have been recommended. What is your name?" "Luigi Capelli." "And you," said we, "are the very man of whom we heard at Lyons." We found Luigi the very prince of guides. Putting ourselves under his care, we were soon landed, and after the usual formalities and extortions at the Custom-house, permitted to go to our hotel on the shore of the bay. Indeed, it seems to me that the Government officials at Naples have reached the very acme of cheating. One wants pay for lifting your trunk; another for touching it; another for looking at it; and still another must be paid for letting it down. And then, having escaped these, you have to encounter a swarm of beggars in all stages of misery, and seemingly with every form of disease. They abound everywhere in Naples, and are so active and pertinacious that it is almost impossible to escape them. A blind beggar, and a lame one, once ran a race with our carriage, coming from Pompeii, and kept up with us for several blocks. The lame man came out second best. Begging is one of the arts of Naples, and is carried to a perfection of which we can have had no idea. It is a great relief to reach our hotel, and hear the bright waters of the Mediterranean murmur at our feet their ceaseless music.

Our first thought is of Pompeii and Herculaneum, and under the direction of Luigi, we are soon on our way thither. We pass through the crowded streets of Naples, filled with a busy bustling population; and what they have to be busy about no one can tell, for there is nothing to do, and yet they contrive to be merry in the midst of misery and want, and with no commerce worth speaking of, manage to give their city the air of a modern metropolis of trade.

They are a nation of Mark Tapleys, and like that character in Dickens' novel, they are jolly under the worst of circumstances. Tapley was to have upon his tomb, "Here lies a man who would have come out strong, but never had the opportunity." The people of Naples *have* the opportunity and they improve it! We make our way out through troops of lazzaroni and beggars; amid donkeys and Neapolitan cabriolets; past companies of soldiers; processions of priests; splendid churches and palaces; squalid and wretched hovels; lovely villas, surrounded by gardens laid out with exquisite taste; long lines of high stone walls, through which may be occasionally seen the entrance to some fine mansion; over a road of lava, the dust of which as it rises behind us is almost intolerable,—out to the beautiful coast of the bay. Before us Vesuvius, with its two peaks, rises to the height of four thousand feet. The road to Pompeii leads by the base of the mountain, through a succession of villages, which seem but a continuation of Naples. As we approach the modern town built over the ruins of Herculaneum, unmistakable signs of the fearful ravages which the eruptions have made, appear in the immense beds of lava which in many places cover the earth to a great depth. From this point the crater of the volcano is visible, and as we look a river of molten lava is pouring forth and threatening to destroy the village at the foot of the mountain. Here, and at intervals along our road, are statues of priests and saints, their hands raised deprecatingly towards the dreaded volcano.

On the 27th of August, A. D., 79, the first recorded eruption of Vesuvius took place. The first *recorded* eruption; for there must have been eruptions before that, the streets of Pompeii being paved with blocks of lava, so ancient that they are worn in ruts by the carriage wheels, and may now be seen just as they were buried on that fatal day. The crater poured forth a flood of lava, which flowed over the city of Herculaneum, and buried it suddenly and forever from sight. At the same time a cloud of water, pumice-stone and ashes arose from the volcano, and, floating over a distance of eight miles, fell upon Pompeii, the abode of wealth, luxury, taste and crime. Of the early history of this city little is known, although the discoveries which have been made in its exhumed portions tell too plainly of a state of morals which must have rivalled that of Sodom and Gomorrah, and sufficiently explain why God should have, in this singular manner, blotted it from the world.

In the year 1748, a peasant who lived above this city of the dead, determined to sink a well in his garden, and thus accidentally discovered a painted chamber, filled with statues and other objects of art. Since then the work of exhumation has gone on at intervals, until about one-fourth of the city is uncovered. And here, let me remark, in order to correct an erroneous impression which I had before I saw Pompeii, and which others may have shared with me, that in visiting it, you do not go down into a cellar. The city was buried in ashes, and all that is required is to cart them out, and the streets appear just as they were eighteen centuries ago. Indeed the whole is so natural, and so like an inhabited city, that you feel as if you had no right there, and that the inhabitants would return in a few moments, and call you to an account for your intrusion. With Herculaneum it is different. There you *do* go down into a cellar, and have to carry a lamp with you. That city was destroyed by lava, and it is a work of the greatest difficulty to cut away the solid rock. At Pompeii, even, the exhumation is not carried forward very rapidly, and it is thought that there are stores of wealth and curiosities yet to be discovered. When some great dignitary arrives at Naples, the King has a new house or two disinterred, and thus the work proceeds.

About three miles of wall, of great solidity and strength, have been traced out. It is built of immense slabs of lava, laid up without cement, and having perfect joints, which are sometimes dovetailed together. This absence of cement is one of the characteristics of Italian architecture, the stones of some of the noblest and most splendid mansions, which have stood for ages, being thus laid up without it.

My first visit was to the ancient amphitheatre, which stands in the south-western angle of the city. It is built in the form of an ellipse, four hundred and thirty by three hundred and thirty-five feet. It could hold about ten thousand persons, and has eighty or ninety vomitories or entrances. It is said that, at the time of the eruption, this theatre was filled with a throng, who readily made their escape into the country. Retracing our steps, we stand within the streets of the city, which are usually narrow. They are paved with blocks of lava, which are everywhere worn into deep ruts by the chariot wheels. The Russ pavement, so much talked about, was an old idea in Pompeii, as were also the raised stepping-stones, for the convenience of pedestrians wishing to cross the streets during a shower. Often there is a narrow footpath of mosaic or stucco.

As the ashes which buried Pompeii are removed, the ancient appearance of the city is at once restored, so that one feels that he is looking upon the same scenes from which the inhabitants fled in terror, nearly 1,800 years ago. The walls of many of the houses are nearly entire, showing every room and garden as they appeared when the city was destroyed. It is impossible to describe the emotions with which one passes through these silent and deserted streets, houses, and temples. The very manners and customs of the people may be distinctly read, and we seem to be introduced into their homes and see how they lived, and what were their pleasures and business. Here are streets of stores, in which merchants trafficked and grew rich. Here are wine-shops, the bottles still unbroken, the name of the owner over the door, the marble-topped tables (no new idea at our restaurants) at which his customers sat, and the very marks of the wine-glasses still upon them. Here are private houses with beautiful gardens and fountains, kitchens, dining-rooms, and sleeping-apartments. Here are floors of rich mosaic, as perfect as when it was first laid. Here are frescoes, and marble statuary, and exquisite carvings, showing a degree of art and skill unsurpassed at the present day. Here are the temples where the people worshipped, the idols to which they sacrificed, and the altars on which they left their offerings. Often the name of the owner is upon his door-post, and we can see where Sallust lived, and where the wealthy Diomede and his family had their home and their graves.

Immediately behind the barracks, which are tasteful and convenient accommodations for the soldiers of Pompeii, stands a Grand Tragic Theatre, built in a semi-circular form, upon the slope of a hill, open to the air, and facing the sea. Every part of it is lined with Parian marble, and although most of the decorations were removed, we can still form an idea of its ancient splendor. It could seat about 5,000 persons, and many of the seats still retain their numbers and divisions, showing that modern janitors and ushers have no new ideas in this respect. The ladies had seats separated from the rest of the audience, and (significant fact!) immediately behind them was the police officer.

Most of the shops of Pompeii were of a single story, open to the street, and closed with a sliding shutter. In front was a counter of stone or brick, elevated by three steps, the better to display the goods. Bakers' shops had small ovens at one end. Drinking saloons were common. A goat indicated a milk-shop. A picture of two men carrying a large bottle, suggested where wine was sold. Two men fighting was the sign of a gladiatorial school—unless they had primary elections in those days, and taught the art of governing the people by rowdies and shoulder-hitters. The school-master's sign was a man whipping a boy, who was trussed up upon another boy's back, showing that for Young Pompeii they had severer discipline than moral suasion.

The dwelling-houses of Pompeii were mostly upon one floor, so that one is a type of all, excepting the additions which taste or wealth might suggest. The ground-floor is the principal part of the house. You enter through an unassuming gateway into a hollow square, where are usually fountains, statuary, and Mosaic pavements. Around this court are the apartments of the family. There is the boudoir of the lady, the library of the husband, a cozy dining-room, and there, under fanciful columns, where the vines crept upon trellis-work, is the table around which the family gathered to take their ease.

That the Pompeians were fond of bathing, is evident from the fact that most perfect arrangements are everywhere met with for supplying the city with water. Splendid marble bath-tubs, vast bathing-houses, substantial aqueducts, pipes underlying the city, with faucets, &c., like our Croton or Ridgewood, indicate the degree of comfort enjoyed in this respect.

One of the most interesting houses in the city lies just out of the Herculaneum gate. It is the villa of Diomed, one of the famous characters in Bulwer's novel of "The Last Days of Pompeii." His house is three stories high, and contains magnificent suites of rooms. In the cellar were found the skeletons of the family, seventeen in number. Near this is a house called the villa of Cicero, on one of the lower stones of which is written, "Sea and fresh water baths, by Marcus Crassus Frugius." Some of the houses you feel disinclined to enter, for it seems as if the family were only absent on a visit, and a figure of a dog seems ready to fly at you, with " *Cave canem*" (beware of the dog) written upon the Mosaic pavement. But you are reassured at the house of the vestals by the word "*Salve*" (welcome).

That the arts had attained great perfection in Pompeii, is evident. The Museum at Naples, devoted to Pompeian relics, contains clothing, bread, fruits, lamps, statues in bronze and marble, dining-sets, paintings, sculptures, &c. The sculptures abundantly testify what life and morals in Pompeii were, and one may easily guess why it was selected to share the fate of Sodom. The decorations of the houses, even the jewelry which women wore, the painting and sculpture now hidden from the public eye, are said to evince a degree of vice, sensuality, and obscenity that rivals the cities of the plains. They evidently worked iniquity with greediness, and realized the portrait of heathenism given by the Apostle Paul in his Epistle to the Romans. Everything about the ruins tells of the suddenness with which the calamity came upon them. There stands a block of marble, half sculptured, and the tools thrown hastily down around it; here is money in the till, and there is freshly plastered mortar, with the down stroke of the trowel only half completed.

Near one of the theatres is the temple of Isis, with its private staircase, by which the priest entered the image and worked the oracle. The winking and weeping Madonnas of the present age are no new ideas. At one of the gates a Roman soldier was found, who remained at his post, careless of threatened danger, faithful to the last. It requires no great stretch of imagination to repeople these silent streets; to recall the hour when the theatre resounded with the applause of thousands; when the temples echoed the sounds of worship; when the shops were filled with merry customers; when that court of justice was the scene of many an eloquent appeal; when the thoroughfares were brilliant with processions, and alive with bustling citizens; when these houses were the abodes of wealth, taste, and most fearful crime.

But in an hour this splendor vanished. Yonder mountain quaked, and its terrible throes and dreadful groans gave appalling evidences of the coming calamity. Then flashed up the long pent-up fires. The molten lava, as a deep, rapid river, poured forth its desolating streams upon Herculaneum. A cloud, dark and ominous, moved towards Pompeii, and fell, and for 1800 years it has laid in its tomb—a lost and buried city.

Retracing our steps towards Naples, we pause at Herculaneum, and, following a guide, descend to the theatre. It is strange, in that deep and dark solitude, where everything carries you back to the past, to hear the tread of active life about you, and to ascend from the graves of the dead city to the realities of the present. You have been carried back over a period of 1800 years. It is difficult to realize that you are living in the nineteenth century. You carry with you those strange thoughts to your evening meditation, and when lulled to slumber by the soft music of the sea, are still dreaming of Diomed, Sallust, and Cicero. You wake to see around you a city full of striking contrasts.

Narrow streets, up which a donkey can scarcely climb, run out from broad and well-paved thoroughfares. Three hundred churches, in a population of 365,000, filled with statuary of wondrous beauty, and superbly decorated, stand in the midst of filthy places, and are surrounded with squalid beggars.

The lazzaroni sleeps in his basket, or in the streets, or under the shadow of a palace, and eats his macaroni at the market-place, and dozes away his life in inaction.

The peasant mounts his donkey, or crowds into the rickety cabriolet, while the noble dashes by in his carriage. The cottage and the palace —the people and the priest—the oppressed and the oppressor, are the terrible contrasts of Naples. You are pointed to relics of superstition of the most puerile character. You see crowds of ignorant and idle people amusing themselves with puppet shows, or listening to the trash of a strolling singer or improvisitoire. But all the noble, earnest and honorable instincts of humanity are crushed out by a bigoted priesthood, and a cruel and tyrannical government that is wholly at its bidding. Yet in these men, now oppressed and down-trodden, the government will at length find the elements of revolution, which will burst forth with a destructive power from which there will be no escape.

I was credibly informed, that in the Neapolitan kingdom there were one hundred thousand families, most of whom were the respectable portion of society, who were deprived of the privileges of a liberal education, from suspicions of their political principles. The object of the Government was, to prevent the spread of heretical opinions by cutting off the children from the power which education might give them to extend and perpetuate the ideas received from their fathers. When such remedies as these are resorted to, it is not difficult to imagine what will be the end of a government already hated and despised, or of the besotted priesthood, who use it as the instrument of their own ambition.

VI.

ROME.

A CROWD of passengers, affording the usual contrasts of a Mediterranean steamer, stood upon the deck of the *Visuvio*, awaiting, for four weary hours, the signal for her departure. Our passports, with four *visas*, for which we had paid the usual extortionate prices, had been brought on board by an officer of the Government, who called off our names, pronouncing them with so thorough an Italian accent, that we were in doubt whether we were really the Signor and Signora intended. However, we stepped up at a venture, and were permitted to remain on board. At length everything was ready, and as the ship shot out from her moorings, we stood upon the deck and gazed on the scene before us, recalling the past few days like some exciting, but beautiful dream. As we sailed up the bay, and evening deepened around us her sombre shadows, Vesuvius was lighted up with its volcanic fires; and when the city of Naples faded from our view, like some beautiful vision, the burning mountain was still our landmark, pointing out to us where lie the buried cities of other ages, and where, perchance, before another year, the earth shall open to swallow up the cities of the present age.

There is a charm about Naples which holds one spell-bound, and the scholar walks under its full power. Yonder is the Sybil's Cave, whose romantic beauty Virgil has rendered immortal in his song. And there is Lake Avernus, upon whose gloomy shore the ghosts of the departed were said to wander; and, above all, there is the spot where Paul landed on his way to Rome, and we are soon to be amid scenes upon which he looked, and among which he was an actor.

A night is spent in dreams of the past and the future, and morning finds us at Civita Vecchia, waiting for permission to go on shore, and when on shore, impatiently anxious to escape from one of the most infamous dens of Italy.

Every conceivable arrangement is made at this place for cheating travellers on their way to Rome. The ship does not land you, but leaves you to the tender mercies of the boatmen. A sailor must be paid for putting your baggage in the boat; the steward and stewardess must be paid for neglecting you during the whole voyage; men must be paid for carrying your baggage to the Custom-house; officers must be feed for inspecting it; one for setting it out of doors, and another for putting it on the omnibus, which demands an exorbitant price for conveying you to the depot, where your baggage is set down at the foot of a flight of stairs, up which a porter must be paid for carrying it, and another for putting it on the cars. It has become a proverb that there is more cheating done and more lies told at Civita Vecchia than in all the rest of Italy; and we only wonder how so many persons are induced to go to Rome, when they have to pass through this purgatory of extortion. At length, after eight hours spent in this nest of thieves [and pickpockets, we are permitted to depart. The railroad, which has been opened but a few months, skirts the shores of the Mediterranean, and passes through a country which, with proper enterprise, might be made a beautiful garden. When former Popes were applied to for permission to build this road, they declined on the ground that then the diligence drivers—some half a dozen vagabonds—would have nothing to do; and so for many years travellers spent from eight to ten hours in journeying forty miles. The present Pope, however, became convinced, by some miracle, that it would not ruin the Church to have a railway to Rome, and so it was finished some two or three months before our visit. At last we came in sight of Rome, and we landed at the station just as the rays of the setting sun were gilding the dome of St. Peter's.

Rome! The Eternal City! I cannot describe the emotions which stirred within me, as I first stood within those walls, and felt that the dreams of my youth were realized. We found excellent accommodations at the Hôtel de l'Angleterre, not far from the famous Corso, the Broadway of Rome. Entering our chamber, we sat down to try and realize that we were in the midst of a city whose history goes back for more than seven hundred years before Christ, and which, both as the metropolis of the Roman Empire and the centre of the Papal Church, has been more connected with the fate of nations than any other.

It was the evening of the feast of Corpus Christi, and torch-light processions, with banners and music, and long lines of priests and monks, were passing beneath our window, and giving us palpable assurance that we were in a Catholic city.

Roma la Grandiosa. Let us place ourselves under the care of Stephano, a most faithful guide, recommended to us by Luigi, at Naples, (we shall find him every morning, with a carriage, to begin our day's explorations,) and go forth, to pass over the grave of Rome's former glory, and to gaze upon the monuments and mausoleums of the mighty dead. Rome lies mostly upon the slope of three or four of the most westerly of the seven hills, and if we stand upon the tower, on the summit of the Capitoline hill, we can take in the general features of the city at a glance. Just south of us are the ruins of the Forum, some fifteen or twenty feet below the present elevation of Rome, but from which the rubbish has been removed, so that we may see the pavement which Cæsar, Cicero and the other celebrated men of their age once trod, and the lofty columns against which, perhaps, they once leaned. Near the Forum is the Arch of Septimus Severus, erected in the year 205, by the Roman Senate, in his honor. Not far away stands the Arch of Titus, erected to commemorate the return of his army from the destruction of Jerusalem, and the most beautiful of all the arches of Rome. It is built of white marble, and is ornamented with bas-reliefs of the priests bearing the vessels of the temple, and walking as captors in the train of the victorious army. Looking still to the south, we see the Arch of Constantine spanning the Via Appia, covered with wondrous illustrations of the victories of the nation under the dominion of the Emperor. As the eye sweeps around, it takes in the blackened wall of the Coliseum, and then the Palatine hill, upon which stand the mighty ruins of the Palace of the Cæsars. The walls of the city were built A. D. 271, and are almost thirteen miles in circuit. The material of which they were constructed is the ancient brick, mixed with stone. Following the outline of the wall, until we look westward, we pass a series of ruins, domes, towers, arches, monuments, palaces, and churches, until at last we pause to admire the wondrous magnificence of St. Peter's, seated upon the Vatican hill, and surrounded by the vast ranges of buildings which make up the palace of the Pope. Behind are distant ranges of hills, and the peaks of the Volscian mountains; and to the south are the vast undulations of the Campagna, a plain ninety miles long by twenty-seven broad; while, nestling among the cloud-capped hills, are beautiful villages, towns, and ancient ruins, and scenes of historic interest, which carry you back to ages almost lost in the shadows of time.

Our first visit was to the Church, or Basilica, of St. John Lateran, for the purpose of seeing a procession in which the Pope was to take part. Next to St. Peter's, this is, perhaps, the most interesting church in Rome, because it is here that the Pope is crowned, and one of the first ceremonies he performs is that of taking possession of this venerable church, dating back to the fourth century. Just opposite is the Babtistry, built by Constantine, in which tradition says that he was baptized, and where stands an urn of green basalt, from which, for many ages, the ceremony of baptism has been performed. Taking our position in front of the magnificent building, we awaited the arrival of the Pope, and watched the cardinals as they drove up. Each cardinal has two carriages for himself and his attendants. The horses are fine animals, of the ancient Roman breed, and their trappings are covered with silver and gold. To each carriage were a driver and three footmen, wearing short clothes, white silk stockings, knee and shoe-buckles, and cocked hats profusely trimmed with silver lace, with which their vests and coats were also lined. The cardinals, as they stepped out in their rustling silks, looked, with all their wealth and splendor, more like princes than like officers of a Church professing to imitate Him who was meek and lowly, and who said, "My Kingdom is not of this world;" and their whole appearance was in striking contrast to the beggars who might be seen around.

But yonder, escorted by files of soldiery, and preceded by a full band of music, comes the Pope. His carriage, drawn by six coal-black horses, is a perfect "wonder." The eye is dazzled with the sheen of scarlet and gold, outshining the trappings of any other monarch on earth, as he passes, by a private gate, into the church, where, already, a vast crowd are gathered, kept in check by lines of soldiery and the ever-present Swiss Guard, the chosen and favored attendants of the Pope, and the detestation of the people. The church itself is a noble edifice, glittering with gold and precious stones, and adorned with paintings and statuary of rare beauty. Down the vast aisles, the rich peals of the organ swelling gloriously through the magnificent arches, advances the procession of the Pope, who comes towards the high altar, seated upon a chair, which is borne upon the shoulders of six or eight men, accompanied by priests having crucifixes and other insignia, and passing by ranks of kneeling soldiers and people, upon whom he graciously bestows his blessing, by making in the air the sign of the cross. Poor man! He is dreadfully tossed about while being thus carried along, and he must feel very uncomfortable. He himself says that it makes him *sea-sick*, and it certainly makes us *sick to see him*. The ceremonies which followed were of the most imposing of the Catholic ritual, and we turned away from them with sorrow, that men should be able to palm upon the people such absurd mummeries as a part of religious worship. Nor was this feeling diminished when we were led through the cloisters and the museum connected with this church. Guided by a priest, we were shown the table upon which the Last Supper was laid. It was enclosed in a glass case, and has, somehow, wonderfully survived the destruction of Jerusalem. We thought that it was burnt up, with many other relics, at that time, but it seems not, for it is at this church, properly identified and on exhibition. There, also, is a column of Pilate's house, and a pillar which was split in two when the veil of the temple was rent. There is also a marble slab—the top of a table—with a hole in it about an inch and a half in diameter, and this is the story about it: There was once a priest, who doubted that the holy wafer did really contain the body of Christ, and, while holding it over the table, he let it fall. A miracle ensued. The wafer was so heavy that it fell quite through this marble slab, and made the hole we see, and then stuck against the leg of the table. Of course, the doubting priest was convinced—how could he be otherwise? There, too, are the stairs up which Christ walked on His way to Pilate's house—and how these were preserved from the destruction of Jerusalem also puzzles us. If you wish to ascend these steps you are required to go on your knees. As our faith in their identity was not excessive, we did not make the ascent. Here Luther was climbing when he thought of that passage of Scripture, "We are justified by *faith*," reflection upon which sowed in his mind the first seeds of the Reformation. In this museum, also, is the marble upon which the soldiers threw lots for Christ's raiment, and many other such notable curiosities.

Leaving the church, and passing down the Via St. Giovanni, by the venerable relics of the Claudian Aqueduct, we approach the vast blackened and shattered walls of the Coliseum, whose shadows carry us backward for ages, through scenes of wondrous tragic interest. It was built in the reign of Vespasian and Titus, 72 and 80, A. D. At its dedication, five thousand wild beasts were let loose in the arena, and slaughtered, and for one hundred days games were held in honor of its completion. For four hundred years after, it was the theatre of gladiatorial spectacles, and cruel and bitter persecutions. Of late years, since it ceased to be used

THE COLISEUM.

for such spectacles, its stones have been taken for building materials—many of the noblest palaces and other edifices of Rome being erected, in part, from its ruins—and yet it seems to have lost none of its vast proportions, although it is said that fully two-thirds of its original material are gone. Its form is an ellipse, 584 by 468 feet; the height of the outer wall is 157 feet; the area covered by it is nearly six acres, and 100,000 people could sit in the vast tiers of seats, and look down upon the scenes below. The sight is overwhelming, as you stand upon the very spot where many a martyr suffered, look up at the vast arches which rise above you, and to the walls blackened by the storms of ages, and think what tales they might tell were they endowed with speech. There is the very arch through which the emperors entered; and the vaulted passages leading to the cells in which the wild beasts were confined, and from which, when maddened with hunger, they were let into the arena upon helpless men, and tender and gentle women, whose only crime was a profession of the religion of Christ. But these scenes have passed, a cross is reared upon the spot, flowers are growing there, and around the arena are placed the statues, usual in Catholic churches, representing the passion of our Lord. Just under the shadows of the Coliseum stands a vast ruin, s shapeless mass, amid which is a garden, green with herbage, and beautiful with flowers and fruits. It stands upon the Palatine Hill, and is about a mile and a half in circuit. It is the ancient palace of the Cæsars, built by Augustus upon the site of the houses of Cicero, Hortensius, Catiline and Claudius. Caligula enlarged it; Nero added to it, and Titus improved and beautified it. Here and there, amid the mass of arches, walls and columns, may be found a room, whose size and form indicate the former glory of the palace: but over it all the ivy climbs, and amid its ruins the owl hoots and the satyr dances.

Those who have made the ruins of Rome their study, divide them into three eras:

The first is the Kingly period, dating back to 752—510, B. C. Of the ruins of this period the most ancient is the Cloaca Maxima, a vast sewer built not long after the foundation of the city, and being now about 2,500 years old. A fine arch of this sewer is seen near the river, with a spring of water just by it, at which the women wash their clothes. The Mamertine prison, to which allusions may be found in the works of Sallust, also belongs to this period. A monk conducts us down a flight of twenty-eight steps into a dark subterranean chamber, beneath which is a small cell built of huge stones, which are held together by iron clamps. The entrance was formerly an aperture in the roof through which prisoners were let down. In this cell Jugurtha was starved to death; and here, by the order of Cicero, the accomplices of Catiline were strangled. Here, probably, Paul was confined, for this was the State prison, and he was a State prisoner. Here, too, the church tradition says that Peter was imprisoned—though there is no scriptural ground for supposing that Peter was ever at Rome—and the priests point out the very pillar to which he was chained, and the spring of water which burst up when he wished to baptize the jailer and his family. There is even a print of his face in the solid rock, when Peter fell back against the wall, and left upon it his exact portrait—a new phase of lithographic art! From this cell Peter escaped, the monks tell you, and ran to a church, where you find a monk ready to accept a fee for showing you the spot where the Apostle met the Saviour, who left the print of his feet in a piece of stone, while telling him that he must go back and be crucified. The priests rather spoil the romance of the affair, however, by telling you that this is not the "real original" stone, as they say in New York, but only a copy, and you are rather inclined to believe, that those who can carve out so perfect a representation of the feet, might also have cut out Peter's profile.

Of the second period, the Consular, there are less interesting relics; but there are some, however, with which all are doubtless familiar. The Appian Way is one of these, a road about fourteen feet broad, paved with smooth square stones, which are still in perfect order, after having been travelled over for two thousand years. This was the great southern military road. By it Paul must have travelled, and from this point he must have caught his first view of Rome, and looked upon the many temples, towers, palaces and columns, the ruins of which still stand, like monuments of the greatness of the city.

The period of the Roman Empire, extending from 30 B. C. to 476 A. C., is richest in the memorials now existing in Rome. During the reign of Augustus, the wealth, splendor and power of the city exceeded any former period; and palaces, theatres, and public edifices and works, whose ruins still remain, were built, in numbers and grandeur surpassing anything ever before attempted. His greatest work was the Pantheon, erected B. C. 26, and it is still in wonderful preservation. Its proportions are exceedingly beautiful; and in spite of all the ravages of time—in spite of the fierce assaults of the Gothic nations, which have left their dreadful traces all over Rome, the Pantheon stands, to-day, perfect and entire. Its portico, which has been pronounced faultless by the noblest architects, is composed of sixteen Corinthian pillars of granite, with capitals of marble, and is one hundred and ten feet long by forty-four deep.

Passing through the bronze doors of the main building, affording an opening of thirty-nine by nineteen feet, we enter the vast solitude within. The building is 142 feet in diameter, and is lighted by an opening in the dome, 143 feet from the pavement. The walls are 20 feet in thickness, and the pavement is of porphyry and other rich stones.

The Pantheon has changed from a heathen temple to a Christian church; the niches, which once held the statues of the gods, are now filled with pictures and images of saints, and services are constantly performed there by the priests of Rome.

But we cannot linger here, for every stone has its story, and we wander amid the terrible ruins of this stricken city, as in a dream. Here is the spot upon which was held the interview between Coriolanus and his mother, when she pleaded with him to spare the city in which he first saw the light. Yonder is the tomb of Pompey, and in that palace is his statue, of which Shakspeare writes:

> "E'en at the base of Pompey's statue,
> Which all the while ran blood,
> Great Cæsar fell."

And antiquarians say that this is the very statue referred to, and that it was removed to this palace from the place where the assassination occurred. Here is the tomb of the Horatii and the Curiatii, and in yonder field they fought and died. That magnificent mausoleum, on the Appian Way, was erected more than nineteen hundred years ago, in memory of Cecilia Metella, the wife of Crassus, and it is still in perfect preservation. Passing by the great Circus, where chariot races took place, and in which 300,000 people could find room, let us return to the city, and visit the Roman Forum, built upon the slope and at the foot of the Capitoline Hill. Here is the modern capitol, erected upon the ruins of the ancient. At the top of the stairs are two colossal statues of Castor and Pollux, standing by the side of their horses. Near by is one of Constantine, found in his baths, and in the centre of this piazza stands the splendid bronze statue of Marcus Aurelius. Michael Angelo was a great admirer of it, and by his directions it was removed to this place from the Lateran church, where, at the coronation of Rienzi, the Last of the Tribunes, it was made to do duty as a fountain, wine spouting from one nostril and water from the other.

Before we enter the museum of the Capitol, let us turn aside, for a moment, to look at the Tarpeian Rock, so famous in the early history of Rome—

> "Tarpeian, fittest goal of Treason's race!
> The promontory whence the traitor's leap
> Cured all ambition!"

It is surrounded by buildings, and upon it is a garden, from which I plucked a flower as a souvenir. At its base the soil has collected so as to detract considerably from its height.

But let us enter the museum of the Capitol. It is filled with the relics of ancient Rome, and presents to us some of the master-pieces of her greatest artists and sculptors. Here stands a colossal statue of Julius Cæsar, and there are busts of Cicero, Brutus, Pompey, Cato, and all the orators, statesmen, and poets, of the golden age of Rome. Here are the creations of Phidias and Praxiteles, and other artists of that day, whose works indicate a degree of refinement which shows that age to have been anything but an era of barbarism. There is that world-renowned statue of the Dying Gladiator, which, once seen, can never be forgotten. Byron has painted this wondrous work of art in verses which almost rival in beauty the statue itself:

> "I see before me the Gladiator lie:
> He leans upon his hand; his manly brow
> Consents to Death, but conquers agony;
> And his droop'd head sinks gradually low,
> And through his side the last drops, ebbing slow
> From the red gash, fall heavy, one by one,
> Like the first of a thunder-shower; and now
> The arena swims around him: he is gone,
> Ere ceased the inhuman shout which hailed the wretch who won.
> He heard it, but he heeded not; his eyes
> Were with his heart, and that was far away.
> He recked not of the life he lost, nor prize;
> But where his rude hut by the Danube lay,
> There were his young barbarians all at play;
> There was their Dacian mother; he, their sire,
> Butchered to make a Roman holiday."
>   CHILDE HAROLD.

In this museum are the sculptures of which

Pliny spoke with so much admiration; the Venus of the Capitol; the bronze wolves and ducks found in some ruins near the Tarpeian Rock; the famous statue of Antinous, discovered in Hadrian's villa; and splendid frescoes and paintings, representing the early scenes of Roman history.

Leaving these scenes, we pause to look at the famous church built upon the ruins of the Temple of Jupiter Capitolanus, dating back to the fourth century. It is filled with paintings and statuary, but its chief attraction is a Doll, said to have been made by a pilgrim from a tree which grew upon the Mount of Olives, and painted by St. Luke while the maker was asleep. This doll is called the Bambino; it is honored as one of the chief miracle-workers of Rome, and its shrine is decorated with many costly offerings. Strange stories are told of its power, especially in healing the maladies of children. Captivated by these tales, so the story goes, a Roman lady determined to have the doll always in her house, so that her children might remain in perfect health. Pretending that one of them was ill, she had the doll brought to her house, and caused a *fac simile* of it to be made—size, form, dress, everything was exactly imitated. The counterfeit she sent back to this church, where it was received with appropriate ceremonies, while the lady retained the genuine Bambino, and went to sleep happy in the belief that she was to have no more sickness among her children. In the middle of the night, the priests at the church were aroused by a knocking at the door, and opening, they found their little doll, the genuine Bambino, who had returned to her temple and her faithful servants. A wonderful image is this! It has a carriage in which to take its airings, and on certain days little children act sacred dramas in its chapel. This is another of the "lying wonders of the man of sin," and we shall notice some others, quite as absurd and silly, by and by. We may visit the church of St. Maria Maggiore, and see a few rough planks, said to be the cradle of the infant Saviour; or the church of St. Sebastian, and find the original marble upon which are the prints of His feet!

But, leaving these, let us ascend to the Pincian Hill, which Napoleon made into a splendid drive, and see the nobility of Rome as they come out for an afternoon ride, and then, walking up the Corso and the streets diverging from it, and gazing upon the fountains, statues, churches, temples, palaces, convents, and monasteries, which rise on every hand, we shall form some just conception of Rome, and acknowledge the propriety with which the Italians call it "*La Grandiosa.*" The suburbs of Rome, besides the numerous ruins you meet at every step, contain some beautiful villas. One of the most perfect of these gems of domestic splendor, the villa Albano, is nestling in a grove of exquisite beauty, and is filled with rich paintings and statuary. It is a grateful relief to turn in thither and wander through those splendid halls and corridors, or saunter through grounds laid out with most exquisite taste, listening to the songs of the birds and the play of the fountains, scenting the sweet breath of the flowers and the shrubbery, and sheltering ourselves from the fierce beams of the summer's sun beneath the green, wide-spreading branches of innumerable trees. How marked the contrast to the streets of the city, where everything tells us of greatness and glory fast passing away forever. Yet, even in this quiet retreat, poverty stares us in the face, for at the gate is a group of wretched beggars, who piteously call upon us for alms. Alas! the spell of the destroyer is upon this once mighty city, and its destiny is clearly foretold in that Word which has written its history, and which points to its overthrow, when the rich men and the great men shall cry— Babylon is fallen, and has become the habitation of devils, the abode of every foul spirit, and the cage of every unclean and hateful bird.

VII.

ROME AND ITS CHURCHES.

ROME is a city of churches. And as day after day introduced me to some new wonder, I began to realize the description given of it among the apocalyptic visions of John at Patmos. Rome, the "Mistress of the World," in her greatness and glory as a heathen city, was but a type of what she was to be as the seat of Papal power and authority. Her splendid temples, built for the worship of false gods, have crumbled to dust, only to be replaced by temples as costly in which the magnificent ceremonies of the Pagan ritual may be reproduced in the Christian worship.

To a population of one hundred and eighty thousand souls, there are three hundred and sixty-four churches, of which seven are Basilicas, capable of containing from five to fifty thousand persons. Connected with the churches and other religious establishments, are four thousand five hundred priests and monks, and nineteen hundred nuns, giving a priest to about every forty, and a nun to about every one thousand persons. During the first three centuries of the Christian era, the church which had been established at Rome (probably by some of those persons who were at Jerusalem during the Pentecostal season, who are spoken of as "strangers of Rome," and who were afterwards confirmed in the faith and order of the gospel by the Apostle Paul) was called upon to endure fierce and bloody persecutions. When Paul came to this great city as the Apostle to the Gentiles, Nero was the Emperor, under whom commenced those bloody persecutions which continued through three centuries, and only ceased when Constantine became a convert to the gospel, and gave to the Christian religion his imperial protection. During all this long period, Christianity could rear but few monuments of its glory and power, and hence it is that the crypts of ancient churches are seldom, if ever, found to date back beyond the fourth century, at which time the Church had begun to feel the growing power of the Papacy, and to experience the truth that the smile of the Cæsars was the frown of Christ. Already, at that time, there had begun to be introduced one and another of those forms and ceremonies copied from the Pagan ritual, to meet the demands for imposing and dramatic forms which might appeal to the senses and teach truth by signs and symbols. When, therefore, the researches of the antiquarians of Rome bring to light, as they occasionally do, some Christian temple, with general features which now appear in the Papal churches, it but proves what all ecclesiastical historians admit, that as early as the fourth century, the evil of which the Apostles warned the churches had become apparent, and that the Mystery of Iniquity was even then working, to develop itself more fully during the seventh century, in the recognition of the Cardinal Bishop of Rome as the Sovereign Pontiff, and, during the eighth century, in the crowning this Pontiff a temporal Prince, thus uniting the Keys of the Church with the Sword of the State, and so consummating that unhallowed union which must everywhere, and in all times, work out evil, and only evil, both to the Church and the State. For a political church, whether Catholic or Protestant, must necessarily be more or less corrupt—and Rome is no exception to this rule.

However, I do not propose to argue upon this subject, but to tell you what I saw of the splendid temples, which began to rise after the cessation of the persecutions, and which, in grandeur and magnificence, find their culmination in that miracle of architectural splendor, St. Peter's.

Leaving our hotel and turning into the Corso, we ride leisurely through that great artery of the city, purposely seeking a circuitous route that we may see some of the strange contrasts which everywhere appear. As we leave the favorite resort of the fashionables of Rome, we catch a view of the shattered and blackened walls of the Coliseum; and then, turning towards the Tiber, we enter the Jews' Quarter, a sad and dark corner of the city, reeking with filth and disease. Passing onward, the scene is strange and novel. Here and there women are at work, surrounded by half-clad children, who seem to have forgotten the use of water. Diminutive donkeys, loaded with panniers filled with fruits and vegetables, are standing in the market-places. Smiths are busy at their sooty forges, or itinerant tinkers are seated before the doors of the houses, patching up dilapidated pans and kettles. Girls with flowers, which they are arranging in bouquets, stand at temporary tables which they have set up at the corners of the streets. Slipshod Israelites, with packs of old clothes, or small boxes of jewelry, shuffle by. Wretched beggars, diseased and starving, stretch out their withered hands and ask for alms. Families, clad in the wild and fantastic garb of their native hills, who have come to sit as models for artists, are gathered upon the doorsteps. Ever and anon there passes a procession of priests, with the symbols of their worship; or of nuns, with their quaint costumes and head-dresses, irresistibly making you smile at their grotesque appearance. Here you meet with youthful students of some Roman college, wearing their peculiar cassock and cap. There a band of Roman soldiers file by you, or a *gendarme* turns up from a by-street, giving you an idea of the constant surveillance under which the city is kept by the Government.

Not far from the Jews' Quarter stand the ruins of the Theatre of Pompey, and hard by is the spot where Cæsar met his fate. Crossing the magnificent bridge of St. Angelo, between two rows of splendid statues, we see before us the ancient mausoleum of Hadrian, and the castle of St. Angelo. Ascending, through dilapidated streets, towards the Vatican Hill, we at length reach the grand Piazza in front of St. Peter's, and looking up at that mountain of hewn stone, we feel (as all do) a sense of disappointment at the size and general appearance of that world-renowned structure, a feeling which, as you soon discover, is the result of lack of power in your mind to adapt itself at once to so stupendous a work of art.

It is approached from the east through a piazza, bounded by semi-circular colonnades, in the centre of which stands the mate of the Column of Luxor, which we saw in the *Place de Concorde* at Paris. On either side of this are beautiful fountains, whose waters are playing night and day. The colonnades are themselves well worthy attention, and enclose an area whose diameter, in its widest point, is seven hundred and eighty-seven feet. The width of these colonnades is fifty-five feet; they are supported by four rows of columns, forty-eight feet high, and stand sufficiently wide apart to admit between them two carriages abreast; the whole number of columns and pilasters is three hundred and forty-eight; and upon the entablatures stand one hundred and ninety-two statues of saints, each twelve feet high. Passing through the piazza, you approach a flight of steps, at the bottom of which are colossal figures of Peter and Paul; and here the colonnades terminate in two galleries, each three hundred and sixty feet long, leading to the vestibule of the church. This flight of steps is one of the first objects which serve to convince you of the vastness of St. Peter's, for it seems to stand just at hand, and you imagine that its distance from the base of the ascent up which you are toiling, is not much greater than that which you have encountered in visiting other churches. Yet, as you advance, the church seems to be no nearer, and when you at length reach its door you find that you have had to walk about three hundred feet from the first step, and that since your carriage entered the piazza, you have passed over one-fourth of a mile. The steps are four hundred feet broad. The façade of the church is three hundred and seventy-nine feet long by one hundred feet high, ornamented with eight Corinthian columns ninety-two feet in length, and nearly nine feet in diameter. Thirteen colossal statues of Christ and the Apostles, eighteen feet high, stand upon the attic, and, diminished by distance, look only the height of ordinary men.

Passing through the first entrance, we stand in the magnificent vestibule which is worthy of the glorious temple to which it leads. It is

468 feet long, 66 high, and 50 feet wide. At either end, seeming in the distance only the size of life, are immense statues of Constantine and Charlemagne. Even here the mind is overwhelmed with the vastness of this portico, and with a foreshadowing of what is to burst upon it when one of those curtains is drawn aside, and we look upon the church itself. It is impossible to convey to your minds the emotions I felt when I beheld that wonderful scene, and which daily and hourly increased within me as I returned again and again from gazing upon one and another of the churches of Rome, beautiful and glorious as many of them are, but only seeming to freshen the wonderful sublimity of this mighty temple. Even Byron, whose heart seldom was stirred by religious emotions, seemed to find here a subject suited to his genius; and though his thoughts are wrapped up in the gorgeous drapery of a poet's utterance, he has given to us a most correct idea of St. Peter's.

> "But thou, of temples old and altars new,
> Standest alone, with nothing like to thee;
> Worthiest of God, the Holy, and the True.
>   .   .   .   . Majesty,

STATISTICAL.

Power, Glory, Strength, and Beauty. all are aisled
In this eternal ark of worship undefiled.
Enter: its grandeur overwhelms thee not;
And why? It is not lessened, but thy mind,
Expanded by the genius of the spot,
Has grown colossal, and can only find
A fit abode wherein appear enshrined
The hopes of immortality; and thou
Shalt one day, if found worthy, so defined,
See thy God face to face, as thou dost, now,
His Holiest of Holies, nor be blasted by His brow.
Thou movest—but increasing with the advance,
Like climbing some great Alp, which still doth rise,
Deceived by its gigantic elegance;
Vastness which grows,—but grows to harmonize—
All musical in its immensities;
Rich marbles,—richer paintings,—shrines where flames
The lamp of Gold,—and haughty Dome which vies
In air with Earth's chief structure, though their frame
Sits in the firm-set ground—and this the clouds must claim."

The church of St. Peter stands over an ancient crypt, built in the time of Constantine, and affirmed by tradition to contain the bones of St. Peter. The present edifice was begun in 1450; the work was afterwards committed to Michael Angelo, under whose direction the church was completed as far as the dome in 1563; and thus the work was carried on until, in 350 years from the time when the design was drawn, the structure was completed, at an expense of $50,000,000, besides the further sum of $1,000,000 spent upon the bells, the sacristy, &c., and $31,000 a year expended in repairs. The church is built in the form of a Latin cross, the centre of which is over the crypt and the tomb of St. Peter. The general dimensions are as follows: length of the nave, 613 feet; of the transept and cross, 446 feet; the height of the ceiling, 152 feet; diameter of the dome, 195 feet to the outer walls, and 139 feet in its interior; height from the pavement to the base of the lantern, 405 feet; to the top of the cross, 448 feet. 50,000 people can easily be accommodated in this vast edifice, and yet leave abundance of room for the priests and ordinary worshippers.

Time would fail us even to enumerate the statues of colossal proportions, and the magnificent mosaics which adorn the walls. And it were as impossible to describe the grandeur of the scene, which grows upon you with every successive visit, and at last, in its overwhelming power and sublimity, takes complete possession of all your senses. You look across the immense space, and see men and women seeming like children. You approach the cherubs which hang out from the walls, holding between them the basin of Holy Water, and they grow to the size of giants, whose wrists you cannot span. You look up at the statues which appear only the size of life, and are told that they are over 20 feet in height. You gaze up at the letters in the dome, and the pen of St. John in the splendid mosaic, and are assured that they are six or seven feet in length. Everything is colossal, and the eye cannot, at one glance, take in the full idea of the grandeur of this interior. You look down through that long vista, and see massive columns, arches, piers, beautiful chapels, splendid statues, and wondrous mosaics, which make you forget all you have before seen of architectural beauty. As you advance towards the great dome, you observe the Baldacchino, or canopy, which stands over the relics of St. Peter, and which is 95 feet high, and supported by four spiral columns.

A flight of stairs leads down to a shrine, before which is a kneeling statue of the Pope, who is represented as praying before the tomb of the

Apostle. Ninety lamps, burning night and day, are hung around the enclosure. Back of this stands the vast tribune, in which hangs the chair of St. Peter, with a bronze covering. During the occupancy of Rome by the French, some one climbed up to the chair, and found upon it the name of an Indian Prince, to whom it probably once belonged. As we approach the High Altar, we see the bronze statue of St. Peter, with its great toe nearly worn off by kisses, and which, upon certain days, is dressed in the robes and tiara of the Pope. The four columns which sustain the dome are 250 feet in circuit, having each two niches, one above the other. In the lower recesses are statues of saints, about 16 feet high, and in the upper are various sacred relics: a handkerchief with the likeness of the Saviour upon it; a piece of the True Cross; the head of St. Andrew, and many others. The walls, chapels, and niches are decorated, not with pictures, but with mosaics of exquisite beauty, having all the delicacy, finish, and expression of the finest paintings, and illustrative of such scenes as the Crucifixion of St.

Peter, the Incredulity of St. Thomas, &c. Sepulchral monuments are scattered over the building, commemorative of Popes, sovereigns, and others, who have been especially distinguished for devotion to the Catholic Church. One of the most beautiful groups is that by Michael Angelo, representing the Mother of Christ, with the body of the Saviour upon her knees. It decorates one of the chapels in the north aisle of the church. Beneath the church is the celebrated crypt, from which ladies are excluded, except upon certain fast days, in which are ancient chapels and cells, containing sepulchral urns of former Popes, and other historical characters.

But if we would obtain a perfect idea of St. Peter's, we must ascend to the roof and the dome. We wind up a broad, spiral staircase of solid stone, and emerge upon the roof, 200 feet from the pavement, where we seem to be entering upon the well-paved street of a city. Here it is we begin to realize the immense proportions of St. Peter's. The domes for lighting the chapels below, and the buildings erected for the accommodation of the workmen, constitute a very respectable street, or rather two streets, of which the centre of the roof is the dividing line. Flights of stairs, between the inner and outer shell of the dome, conduct us to its summit, whence we mount by a ladder into the ball, which, although eight feet in diameter, looks like a speck from the street, 450 feet below. As we descend, we pause to look down from the vast galleries upon the pavement beneath, and the crowds of men and women appear but as the moving figures of a puppet show.

The services and ceremonies of St. Peter's are in keeping with its architectural character. Here we witnessed the procession of the Pope, as, borne upon the shoulders of his men, and followed by an immense crowd of cardinals and priests, he passed through files of armed soldiers and a vast throng of spectators, which, though numbered by thousands and tens of thousands, yet left space enough unoccupied to have accommodated as many more. Just at the close of day I attended Vespers, at which the Pope was present, and heard such music swelling through the vast arches of this temple as seldom falls upon the ears of man, this side Heaven.

Adjoining St. Peter's is the Vatican, or Palace of the Pope. It contains over four thousand five hundred rooms, and exceeds in interest and splendor all the other palaces of the world. Its length is about twelve hundred and its breadth about seven hundred and sixty-seven feet. Its various stories are reached by eight grand staircases, and two hundred smaller ones. It would be useless to attempt any minute or detailed description of this vast edifice; yet a few hints may not be inappropriate. Ascending towards it through the left portico of the church, you enter through the grand staircase, which leads to the Sixtine Chapel, a lofty hall, one hundred and thirty-five by forty-five feet, decorated with splendid paintings, the most wonderful of which is the fresco of the Last Judgment, by Michael Angelo. It represents Christ, surrounded by His saints and angels, on the one hand, while beneath Him are the lost spirits descending to their eternal home. Among these is the figure of a cardinal, who objected to the picture, on account of the nudity of the figures, and whom Angelo painted in hell, with asses' ears. When the cardinal complained to the Pope, his answer was, that although his Holiness could deliver him from purgatory, his power did not extend to the lower hell. Passing from this chapel, we proceed through an almost endless series of rooms, museums, and libraries, devoted to the architectural and artistic riches of the world. A vast corridor, seven hundred feet long, is filled with inscriptions, sarcophagi, funeral altars, &c., and contains the finest collection of the kind in the world. Another series of halls has seven hundred specimens of ancient sculptures, where we behold the images of the deities and heroes of ancient Rome, many of them as fresh as when they came from the hands of the artist. Other museums are filled with vast collections of books and manuscripts, of ancient art, of natural history, and of science. The Etruscan and the Egyptian museums are alone worth the study of months; while galleries of sculpture contain some of the noblest works of ancient and modern art. Here stands Apollo, the very personification of manly beauty, watching the flight of the arrow which has just left his hand. Elsewhere we came upon the group of Laocoon, on which Virgil looked, and from which he drew inspiration. We wandered for hours amid these varied collections, lost in wonder at their extent and magnificence, and gaining some new ideas of the wealth which the nations have poured in upon this great city.

Turning from this palace, which holds us with a wonderful fascination, we take our places, just as the sun is setting beneath the softened glories of an Italian sky, to witness the splendid spectacle of the illumination of St. Peter's. Five hundred men are hanging four thousand lanterns upon the columns, arches and windows of the vast edifice, which, in the growing darkness, shine with increasing brightness. Just as the bell strikes the quarter-past nine, one thousand more torches are lighted, and the heavens seem to reflect the glowing splendor like that of a new sun. We gaze upon the scene with astonishment which cannot be expressed, and turning away from that vast crowd of princes, soldiers, priests, and civilians, we pass towards our hotel, finding everywhere the houses and churches reflecting the light of that brilliant illumination, while out in the evening sky hangs that wondrous dome, shining like another sun in its dazzling glory. And yet all this is but in keeping with the wealth and splendor of the Romish Church, which has gathered to itself the riches and grandeur of the nations.

Rome abounds in relics. Beyond the church of St. Paul is a church of the Fountain which sprang up when his head bounded there from the hands of the executioner. Elsewhere you meet with the gridiron of St. Lawrence; a part of the garments of the Virgin and of Christ's girdle; the rod and sponge used at the crucifixion; part of the Virgin's sepulchre; a picture of Christ, given by Peter to Prudens; part of the towel used in wiping the disciples' feet; some of Christ's swaddling clothes and of His seamless vestment; three thorns from His crown; fragments of the true cross, and hundreds of others of the same character. At Rome you meet at almost every church offers of plenary indulgence for the living and the dead. The Church cannot deny that she sells, and has sold, indulgences or premiums to rob, to murder, to commit crimes worse than these. For there is above her church doors: "*Plenary indulgence for the living and the dead.*"

As to the people of Rome, we cannot but observe the seriousness which pervades the whole city, and which strangely contrasts with the mirth and jollity which is seen in Naples, even amid all its poverty. The Romans look serious and gloomy, and well they may. What will be the end of this wondrous city we can only tell by the light of Scripture. If, as there can be no doubt, this is the "Babylon" of the Revelations, then its fate is clearly foretold and distinctly and indisputably described in the language of the Spirit to St. John, as he showed to him the things which must shortly come to pass:

"The merchants of these things, which were

made rich by her, shall stand afar off for the fear of her torment, weeping and wailing, and saying, Alas, alas, that great city, that was clothed with fine linen, and purple, and scarlet, and decked with gold, and precious stones, and pearls! For in one hour so great riches has come to nought.

"Rejoice over her, thou heaven, and ye holy apostles and prophets; for God hath avenged you on her!"

VIII.

ROME TO FLORENCE.

THERE was a wondrous fascination about the city of Rome, which made us linger there, even when we were warned that it was time for us to leave for other scenes. Entering our carriage at an early hour, we passed the morning of our departure in visiting some of the most important and imposing sights of the Eternal City. I have said nothing, because of lack of time, in regard to one of the most beautiful features of Rome—its fountains, which seem to empty a river into the very heart of the city. Here a great sea-monster is spouting the water from his cavernous throat —or dolphins are playing within their marble reservoirs—or Neptune, with his huge horses, is rising from the sea, amid showers of spray

—or a river is pouring forth its singing waters in lovely cascades, over moss-grown rocks. These fountains are a striking feature of Rome, add greatly to its beauty, and stand in living and pleasant contrast to the stern and solemn monuments of the past, whose giant shadows fall upon the city like the ghosts of departed ages.

But we must leave these scenes, where we have been living among the dead of other centuries. Every step brings back some memory of the regal or imperial splendors of this mighty city. Every fallen column, or gigantic ruin, seems a hand thrust out to push back the shadows on the dial of Time. We again gaze upon the blackened walls of the Coliseum, and re-people them with the tens of thousands who once looked upon scenes, the recital of which, even now, thrills the soul with horror. We pass the Forum, and the Capitol; see Cæsar walking in his pride, and Brutus, with his stern, unbending purpose, and hear the voices of the orators of Rome ringing out, clear and distinct, the noble utterances of the advocate or the patriot. We look up once more at that wondrous church which, in magnificence and grandeur, surpasses all other temples made with hands, and think of the history and the destiny of that great hierarchy and spiritual despotism, whose home is there. We pass crowds of priests, nuns, and monks, soldiers and beggars, and wonder if there is not a mutual connection between Popery, Despotism, and Poverty. We go out of the gate of the city, enter the cars, and are whirled away towards the sea; and, as we look back upon the pinnacles and domes of Rome, and see it fading in the distance, like some wonderful vision, we feel that the wild dream of our youth has been realized; that we have looked upon the Eternal City, have wandered amid its monuments, and felt the spell with which it must ever bind both the mind and the heart.

For a strange and mysterious awe hangs over Rome. There it has stood for twenty-five hundred years, amid revolutions which have shaken down and raised up kingdoms. It has seen the race of kings swept away when Tarquin the Proud yielded to the avenger of Lucretia's honor. It has witnessed the destruction of the Republic, and, amid the glories of the Empire, it was adorned with monuments which still speak of its greatness and grandeur. It has been the home of Genius: there the poets sang, the orators spake out "thoughts that breathe and words that burn;" and the painters and sculptors made their art glorious. Time has been busy with its noblest monuments. Hordes of barbarians rushed through its streets, and poured upon its people the red tide of war. Internal dissensions have threatened it with ruin. And yet it still stands, the mausoleum of its own greatness, awaiting the time when God's threatenings shall be fulfilled, and the blood of the saints, there poured out, shall be most fearfully avenged. And its fall, with that of the system of religious intolerance, oppression and superstition inseparably connected with it, shall be the rising from the dead, both of Italy and the world.

But, not to linger longer among these scenes, once more we find ourselves at Civita Vecchia, awaiting permission to go on board the steamer, which has stopped for passengers just within the harbor. When the last extortionate demand is at length satisfied, we stand upon the deck of the steamer, and wonder if Civita Vecchia has its equal in the world for rascality and for all mercenary appliances, with which to put to the severest possible test the ordinary virtues of humanity.

A crowd of passengers are on board the steamer, among whom are some Americans, whom, as they will be our companions over the Alps, we may as well introduce at once. That gentleman, with a merry eye and slouched hat, is our former fellow-citizen, the artist Rogers, who has attained an enviable position as a sculptor, and having just finished and sent off his models for the bronze doors of the Capitol at Washington, is now resting, for a few days, from study. The ladies are from the sunny South, and although one is a Roman Catholic, she has so much of the true stamp of piety, both in her manner and conversation, that you cannot help loving her. There are two princesses on board, entire contrasts in appearance. The one is young, beautiful and lovely. The other neither young nor beautiful. Priests and monks, some with black serge cassocks, others in white flannel, and others still, with coarse sackcloth robes, whose hoods are drawn over their heads in lieu of hats, swarm around, their toes and heels sticking out from toeless and heelless sandals; and what possible connection there is between religion and the wearing of dilapidated shoes and grotesque apparel, I could never understand. Crowds of travellers returning from Naples, Malta and Rome, are sitting in groups about the deck, while the sailors are busily covering with tarpaulin the heaps of baggage upon the deck, anticipating the rain which yonder clouds threaten.

A night of utter discomfort passes, and morning finds us at Leghorn, one of the ports of Tuscany, where the stranger is totally abandoned to the tender mercies of boatmen and commissioners. We are rowed to the Customhouse and Police station, which stands upon an island, and from thence we reached the main land, where the most prominent object is the celebrated statue of the Four Slaves, executed in honor of Ferdinand de Medici. Here we meet the galleys, one of the first objects which strike the stranger in the Mediterranean ports, where the Government prisoners are employed, instead of donkeys or steam engines, to load and unload vessels.

Leghorn is the commercial capital of Tuscany, and has every appearance of thrift and prosperity. It is a favorite summer resort of the Italians, and the drive along the shore is one of great interest and beauty. On the one hand sleep the blue waters of the Mediterranean; on the other are beautiful villas, surrounded by exquisite gardens and shrubbery, and giving evidences of domestic comfort and ease widely contrasting with the poverty and filth which may readily be found in other parts of the city.

After a thorough examination of our baggage and passports, we find our way to the cars, and in an hour's ride through a pleasant farming country, are set down at Pisa, one of the most ancient and beautiful towns in Italy, situated in the midst of a fertile plain, about eight miles from the sea. The river Arno divides the city into two unequal portions. The streets are narrow, and are crowded with a population which seems to live wholly out of doors. Priests, soldiers, monks, *gendarmes*, nuns, donkeys, beggars, women and children, busy or idle, driving bargains, or lounging in utter listlessness, selling flowers or fruits, or running after the carriage for a few *granos*—these make up the crowd through which you pass, on your way to the north-western extremity of the city, where the great attraction of Pisa is to be found. Emerging from the narrow streets into an open square, we come to the cathedral, with its campanile, baptistry, and celebrated burial-ground.

The first object which attracts our attention is the Leaning Tower. It is probable that before it was finished, the foundation on one side began to sink, and to overcome this difficulty, the columns on the leaning side were made larger than those opposite. Yet still the tower, although one hundred and eighty feet high, inclines so far, that a line dropped from its summit would fall fifteen feet from the base. It is a graceful structure, light and airy, eight stories high, and supported by two hundred and seven columns. In the seventh story is a chime of bells, one of which weighs ten thousand pounds. It was here that Galileo made his experiments to discover the laws of falling bodies.

Crossing to the cathedral, we enter one of the finest churches in Italy, enriched by spoils taken from the Saracens, and supported by columns which once stood in ancient structures in Rome, Greece and Egypt. It is built in the form of a cross, three hundred and eleven by two hundred and thirty-seven feet; and was begun in the year 1067, and finished in 1118. Its interior is singularly rich and beautiful. Two rows of Corinthian columns—twelve on either side—of red granite and various marbles, form a base, from which springs a series of beautiful and airy arches, rising to and supporting the ceiling, ninety-one feet from the pavement. One of the altars is of Lapis Lazuli, the costliest stone of Europe; another is encased in silver, while statues of solid silver support the tabernacle, and give to the whole an air of richness which few, if any others in the world, can equal. From the ceiling still hangs the bronze lamp, whose vibrations first suggested to Galileo the idea of the pendulum. Passing out through the bronze doors of the cathedral, we enter the baptistry, a building ninety feet in diameter, with a dome one hundred and eighty feet in height. In this structure is a most wonderful and perfect echo, by which a few notes of music are caught up, repeated and multiplied, until they die away in the recesses of the dome, as if angels had caught the melody and were bearing it heavenward. Near the baptistry is the Campo Sancto, or burying-ground, which was fitted to be the repository of the dead by being filled with fifty-three vessel loads of earth brought from Mount Calvary. Beautiful frescoes by Giotto adorn the walls, while around are sarcophagi, urns, vases and statues of rare interest and beauty. This Giotto was a celebrated Italian artist, and when a deputation from the Pope came to him to ask him for a specimen of his skill, so that the Church might judge whether he was able to paint her frescoes, he simply drew a circle, and said, "Take that." "Is this all?" asked the messengers. "It is enough," replied Giotto. It *was* enough, and Giotto went to Rome. In this burial-place you see the tombs of many of the noblest families in Italy, appropriately adorned with statues or bas-reliefs.

But leaving Pisa, we again take the road from Leghorn to Florence, which is about fifty miles in length, and runs through a well-cultivated valley, watered by the Arno, and bounded by ranges of hills that increase in height as they approach Florence, where they close in about that city and present from their summit one of the loveliest panoramas in Italy. The valleys and hill-sides, between Leghorn and Florence, are covered with fine crops of grain, with vineyards, and olive-yards, whose luxuriance promises an abundant harvest; while large patches of flax are strewed along the Arno, undergoing the processes by which they will soon be transformed into thread and cloth. The fields are filled with joyous groups of happy peasants, male and female, who are securing the rich harvests which have whitened beneath the summer's sun. At the doors of their neat cottages, or beneath the cool shade of the trees or widespreading vines, women and children are busy with their distaffs and spindles, or plaiting the braids of straw which form so important an article of commerce in Tuscany. The distaff is the same which has been in use for thousands of years in the East, and brings back to the mind the customs of the ancients. There is another custom which, ever since Jacob kissed Rachel at the well, has become quite universal and popular as a sign of affection between the sexes; but we do not often see men kissing men. On our way to Florence, however, we witnessed this (to us) strange spectacle, and although we have adopted many foreign fashions, I presume this will not soon become general. Two men, neither of whom were very small, and one was immense, happened to meet in the cars, and, throwing their arms about each other with the greatest gusto, gave such a smack that one would have thought the cars had broken down. This method of salutation is quite common in Italy.

As we approach Florence, the scenery increases in beauty, till we at last enter the city, and proceed to the delightful Hotel of Madame Molini, in the old Palazza Schneideriff. We entered Madame Molini's house strangers, and eft it as friends, with, we trust, mutual regret. The walls of Florence, six miles in circuit, enclose a population of about one hundred and sixteen thousand souls. The river Arno divides the city into two unequal parts, the largest of which lies northward of the river. Four bridges cross the Arno within the city limits, and two in the suburbs. One of these bridges, the Ponte Vecchio, seems like a street, and, indeed, is only the continuation of one, and is lined with shops, mostly for the sale of jewelry, of which the people are extravagantly fond, scarcely a peasant girl appearing without at least a string of gold beads, which have been in her family perhaps for generations. The Ponte di Santa Trinita, a beautiful marble bridge, having three noble arches, is decorated at each extreme with statues of the seasons, and is about three hundred and twenty-three feet long. This is about the width of the Arno, which is so shallow that one can wade across it anywhere.

Crossing this bridge, or the Ponte Vecchio, we pass through various streets, lined with shops of every description, and thronged with a busy and active population, who give every evidence of thrift and industry. We entered Florence not long after the revolution which followed the abdication of the Grand Duke, who foolishly threw himself into the arms of Austria. Yet everything was moving on under the provisional government as peacefully as if the people had been accustomed to self-government for years—a noble evidence of the character of the Italians, and their fitness to enjoy the blessing of a free and liberal government, if but left to themselves. When the Grand Duke abdicated, there was no shouting, no open rejoicing, no popular outbreak—the people behaved like gentlemen, and concealed the exultation they felt. Neither did they abuse their power.

All the officers of the Court, except those who were Austrians, were retained in their stations, and they did not, as we do, turn out tried and faithful servants, because they do not happen to vote the same ticket, or believe the same set of political opinions that we do.

Every day's sojourn in Florence gives us a new impression of the appellation, "*Firenze la Bella,*" Florence the Beautiful! Genius and wealth have left their enduring monuments on every hand. First in interest and grandeur is the Duomo, or cathedral, whose outer walls are encased in rich Italian marbles, and whose massive and magnificent dome gave to Michael Angelo the idea of that of St. Peter's. The interior is sombre and dark, on account of the small windows and stained glass, but the effect is grand and sublime, as you stand beneath the swelling dome and look down through the vast arches and columns, and hear the glorious music which rises heavenward at morning and evening service. The walls and ceilings are comparatively bare of decorations. Here is the celebrated, though unfinished, picture by Angelo, of the entombment of Christ; and here repose the ashes of Giotto. Near the church stands the campanile, a square tower of marble, elaborately wrought, and rising to the height of two hundred and seventy-five feet. So rich and beautiful is this bell-tower, that Charles V. declared that it ought not to stand out of doors, but should be kept in a glass case, to be exhibited only on special occasions.

Just opposite is the baptistry of San Giovanni, entered by immense bronze doors, on which are wrought scripture scenes, in bas-relief, so perfect that Michael Angelo, and, after him, the poet Rogers, declared that they were fit to be the gates of paradise. This baptistry is supposed to have been built as early as the seventh century, and was for many years, until the erection of the Duomo, used as a cathedral church. All of the baptisms of the city are performed here. But the church of most interest is that of Santa Croce, the Westminster Abbey of Italy. As you pass up and down the vast aisles and through the numerous chapels of this church, you meet with names whose fame is world-wide and undying. Here is the tomb of Michael Angelo, placed, as he desired, so that when the doors of the church are open, the cupola of the Duomo may be distinctly seen. Here stands a statue of Italy, pointing to the image of Dante, whose ashes sleep in exile from the home of his youth. Here are the monuments to Galileo, who was treated as a heretic, until they found that the world would not regard him as such; of Alfieri; of Michielli and Boccacio. Here sleep the wife and daughter of Joseph Bonaparte; and here are interred the ashes of the father of the present Emperor of France. Many of the monuments and tombs are of the most exquisite and perfect workmanship, rivalling life, or rather death itself, in their cold loveliness.

Not far from the Duomo is the church of Santa Maria Novella, which Angelo used to call "his bride, and his dear delight." Here Boccacio used to meditate, and here he arranged the opening scenes of his "Decameron," during the prevalence of the plague. On the whole, there is, perhaps, no church in Florence which combines so much of interest and beauty as this. The decorations are scarcely equalled in Italy for wealth and exquisite taste. Here is the celebrated Madonna, painted upon a ground of gold, and representing the Virgin with the infant Saviour, surrounded by angels. The rival of this church is that of the Annunciation, containing the wonderful picture of "the Annunciation," said to have been painted by the angels while the artist was asleep. Near by is the church of San Lorenzo, consecrated in the year 393, by St. Ambrose, but rebuilt in the thirteenth century. Its chief interest is derived from the buildings connected with it, in one of which is the famous library, built by the Medici family, and containing upwards of nine thousand manuscripts alone, of the rarest character. Besides autographs of Virgil, and other Roman poets, there are Egyptian, Hebrew and Chaldaic manuscripts, precious beyond price.

The sacristy is one of the first works of Michael Angelo as an architect. This is

"That chamber of the dead,
Where the gigantic shapes of Night and Day,
Turned into stone, rest everlastingly."

Here are the sepulchral monuments of the Médicis, and other noble families of Tuscany. Upon one of them, containing the remains of Lorenzo de Médicis, there are two figures representing Morning and Twilight; and immediately opposite are the statues of Night and Day, which, though unfinished, are sufficiently advanced to allow us to see the magnificent conception of the artist who could think out the Last Judgment and the cathedral of St. Peter's. Over these the statue of Lorenzo is seated. He appears absorbed in thought, resting his face upon his hand, by which it is partially covered. The light, as it falls upon this figure, throws upon it a peculiar shadow which gives to it a mysterious and almost painful fascination. Rogers, the poet, alludes to it in his " Italy," in terms which have doubtless found a response from many a visitor, who has gazed upon and dreamed of that weird statue.

> "What, from beneath this helm-like bonnet, scowls?
> Is it a face, or but an eyeless skull?
> 'Tis lost in shade; yet, like the basilisk,
> It fascinates, and is intolerable."

This statue also is by Michael Angelo, whose

name we have repeated often, but not half so often as one is obliged to listen to in Italy. You look upon some graceful and beautiful sculpture, and ask whose work it was: "Michael Angelo's." Presently, in some other place, you happen upon a figure which fairly enchants you. If you ask whose it is you have the same reply—"Michael Angelo's." You see some chapel exquisitely designed and built, and ask the architect: "Michael Angelo." You find a figure of Moses, coming up to your idea of what Moses really was—the sculptor was Michael Angelo. Finally, you go to St. Peter's, that wonder of the world, that mountain of hewn stone, and you feel that it is a fit monument for such a man, whose mind sported with conceptions which would have crushed any ordinary intellect, and seemed to delight in the immense and massive. Angelo was a sculptor and painter, as well as an architect, and it is said that he could paint with one hand while sculpturing with the other.

We next enter the Medicean Chapel, which was designed as a mausoleum for the Medicean family, a race which has now altogether died out. Upon the escutcheon of this family are the three golden balls, now seen before pawnbrokers' shops. The merchants of Lombardy, many of whom were pawnbrokers, adopted this sign, and it has now become general. To return, however, the chapel is lined with rich Mosaics, of mother-of-pearl, topaz, coral, cornelian, chalcedony, agate, lapiz lazuli, and others of the most precious stones, fitted together with the most exquisite taste and skill. The chapel is slowly advancing towards completion, although often delayed for want of means, or by political disturbances.

From the brief and imperfect description we have given of the churches, you may form some idea of what the palaces must be. Let us visit the Palazza Vecchio, the seat of the ancient government of Tuscany. In front of it are groups of statuary of the most interesting character: one is Hercules, another the David of Angelo. Under a lofty arcade is the "Rape of the Sabines," and "Perseus," and near by is a magnificent bronze statue of Cosimo I. Entering the Palace, we pass through vast saloons, containing the masterpieces of the world. Here is the famous Venus de Medicis, whose beauty Byron has sung:

> "We gaze, and turn away, and know not where;
> Dazzled and drunk with beauty, till the heart
> Reels with its fullness; then forever there,
> Chained to the chariot of triumphal art,
> We stand a captive, and would not depart."

In the same room are other groups of statuary, and exquisite paintings by Raphael, Titian, Paul Veronese, Vandyck, Del Sarto, and a host of others, whose works have made their names immortal. Here, day after day, we stand and gaze at these magnificent conceptions of the Masters of Italy and the world, and understand, better than ever before, the meaning of the verse:

> "A thing of beauty is a joy for ever."

Nor is our amazement at the extent and power of Italian genius lessened when we cross the Arno, and wander through the magnificent halls of the Pitti palace, with its profusion of paintings and statuary, of which time would fail us to speak. Indeed, there seems to be no end of the palaces and museums of Florence. Here is a noble collection of Natural History. A suit of rooms has been appropriated to the instruments with which Galileo carried on his investigations into the laws of the universe. Here, in three glass cases, is a most wonderful representation of the progress of death by the plague, from the first symptoms of the disease to the last stages of decay. One wonders how the artist ever modelled these figures without himself catching the plague.

Nor does Florence lose its interest, as we pass to its suburbs. On that hill, just south of the city, rises the tower from which Galileo studied the heavens, and where Milton visited him in his retirement; and still beyond is the house where the philosopher, neglected, outcast and persecuted, died in poverty, attended only by a single friend.

From what has been said of Florence, as a repository of art, it is no wonder that it is the home of artists. Here Powers lives, and at his studio we saw the statue of Washington, recently arrived in this country, and the exquisite figure of "California." Hart, of Kentucky, and many other American and foreign sculptors have their studios here.

Passing out of Florence, we ascend the heights of Fiesole, with its ancient Etruscan walls, and the old town and fortress, rising 1,100 feet above the city, and which stood before Florence was built. Here is a Franciscan monastery, and many interesting relics of the aborigines of Tuscany. As you look from the hill, one of the lovliest of panoramas is before you. A large city, with its Italian towers and domes, is at your feet, surrounded by an endless variety of beauty; while beyond, the swelling hills, crowned with groves of olives, vineyards, and smiling villas, form a background to a picture which, once seen, can never be forgotten.

Florence abounds in public gardens and drives, of which the most remarkable are the gardens connected with the Pitti Palace and the Cascino. The former are, perhaps, the most beautiful and extensive in Europe. They are exquisitely laid out upon the hills overlooking the city, and have scattered along their walks 5,000 vases of flowers, and 500 citron and orange trees. The Cascino, lying west of the city, upon the Arno, is a vast park where the citizens meet of an afternoon for social recreation and enjoyment. Fashionable calls are made upon the ladies as they sit here in their carriages.

Among the many benevolent institutions of the city is the Misericordia, a society formed to give relief to the sick and dying. A call of the bell brings together the members, who are disguised in black gowns, dominos, and masks, and who, without recognizing each other—so that a gentleman may stand side by side with his valet—meet to perform the duties of their office. It is no uncommon thing of an evening to see a procession of the members of this society, having a litter with some sick or wounded man upon it, whom they are bearing to the hospital or his home, there to be attended to until returning health or death releases him from his sufferings.

While Florence and Tuscany are both Roman Catholic, and feel the full power of the priesthood, it is a fact which cannot but elicit the gratitude of every Christian, that there the gospel has been preached, and has found a foothold; that Protestant ministers and churches have been tolerated to some extent, and that nearly 10,000 copies of the Bible have been put in circulation. The Bible-readers abound there, and carry on their operations as at Lyons. Inquiry after the truth has been awakened, and we cannot but trust with confidence in workings of that Word, of which God has said, "It shall not return unto me void."

IX.

FLORENCE TO TURIN.

WE left Florence with regret. Who could suppress a sigh at bidding farewell to a city of such beauty, to scenes where nature has fairly lavished her loveliness, and to friends whose kindness had made us a home, even in a land of strangers. We were turning away from the abode of Genius and Art; from scenes which have been made forever memorable by the chisel of the sculptor, the pencil of the painter, the lyre of the poet, and the pen of the historian. It was on the morning of a beautiful summer day that we took leave of that group of friends whom we had daily met at the table of Madame Molini, and drove towards the station on the road to Leghorn. A flood of golden sunlight was streaming down upon that lovely valley in which Florence rests, and bathing in glory the swelling hills which surround the city. On our right rose abruptly the heights of Fiesole, with its monastery, designed by Michael Angelo, its lofty and imposing cathedral, and its quaint commingling of ancient and modern architecture. Behind us was the hill, crowned with the antique tower from which Galileo once explored the heavens with his telescope; while still beyond it were the forests and mountains of Vallambrosa. Upon our left were the bright waters of the Arno, while on every side the hills were smiling in their beauty, covered with thousands of villas and palaces, looking out from dense groves of olives and cypress, or surrounded by fields stacked with the gathered harvest, or giving promise of a rich and abundant vintage. Here and there a crumbling ruin, an abandoned fortress, or a time-worn cathedral, pointed us back to ages of past glory, which filled Italy with its monuments; while the vast dome of the Santa Maria, with its beautiful campanile (whose bells were even then summoning the Florentines to their matin devotions), once more arrested our attention, and seemed to impress indelibly upon our memories the beauties which were fast fading from our visions.

As we recall even now that scene of exquisite loveliness, we can fully sympathize with the impassioned words of Byron, who once visited these scenes, whose genius kindled beneath their wondrous beauty, and whose mind and heart appreciated the terrible reality of Italy's oppression and suffering:

> "Italia! Oh, Italia! Thou who hast
> The fatal gift of beauty, which became
> A funeral dower of present woes and past;
> On thy sweet brow is sorrow plough'd by shame,
> And annals graved in characters of flame!
> Oh, God! that thou wert in thy nakedness
> Less lovely or more powerful, and could'st claim
> Thy right, and awe the robbers back, who press
> To shed thy blood, and drink the tears of thy distress;
>
> "Then might'st thou more appall; or, less desired,
> Be homely and be peaceful, undeplored
> For thy destructive charms; then, still untired,
> Would not be seen the armed torrents pour'd
> Down the deep Alps; nor would the hostile horde
> Of many-nation'd spoilers from the Po
> Quaff blood and water; nor the stranger's sword
> Be thy sad weapon of defence, and so
> Victor or vanquish'd, thou the slave of friend or foe."

No man can tread amid the fair scenes of Italy, and not feel a pang of sorrow that, with so much that is lovely and glorious in Nature and Art, there should be everywhere present the marks of oppression and superstition. When shall Italy rise in her power and dignity as a nation? When shall the light of God's Word scatter the midnight that now rests with its dark and gloomy shadow over scenes of such exquisite beauty, and over a people who, under proper influences, might reproduce the old Roman glory, heightened and made perpetual by the light of a true and spiritual religion. The Papal Church,—with its load of superstitions and childish mummeries, its idle traditions, its unscriptural rites and doctrines, its armies of priests, monks, and nuns; its vast monastic institutions; its wily and terrible Jesuitism, and its hatred of the Word of God as a Book for the people,—rests like a nightmare upon Italy. It opposes her progress; it interferes with her political institutions; it winds itself into her government; it arrays her kings and princes against her citizens; it shuts out light and liberty; it loves darkness and resists every effort to scatter its shadows. In her recent struggle to free herself from the dominion of Austria, and to give her fair domain to her own children, Italy has found her bitterest opponent in the Roman hierarchy. Can we doubt that, when the day of retribution comes—as come it will—all this will be remembered, and the voice which John heard in Apocalyptic vision shall be echoed over the plains of Italy, heralding the downfall of the terrible system which has so long crushed out the liberties of the world, "Reward her as she has rewarded you?"

But we must hasten on from these scenes and reflections. A pleasant ride of three hours brings us to Leghorn, where, after the usual delay, we find ourselves on board the "Vatican," with an immense throng of passengers, waiting for three long and weary hours the departure of the steamer. Just before sunset we made our way out of the harbor, and were again afloat upon the blue waters of the Mediterranean, and gazing upon the distant hills along the coast, which were shining in the indescribable glow of an Italian atmosphere. The crowded state of the ship excluded all hope of obtaining any ordinary sleeping-place, and afforded us the opportunity of seeing every available spot upon the quarter-deck covered with mattresses, and some fifty or sixty men, women and children, priests, monks and nuns, undertaking to sleep through a night of heat so intense as to be almost unendurable. My friend Rogers and myself made our way forward, through a mass of heads, arms and feet, so intermingled that it required skilful navigation to avoid treading upon them, and found a most comfortable standing-place, where we could while away an hour in talking of Italy, her past, present and future. Toward morning I crept into the cabin and attempted to sleep, but it was like trying to keep cool at the mouth of a furnace. The morning at length dawned, and with its first grey twilight I arose and looked out upon the hills of the Bay of Genoa.

The light had not yet gone out in the tower which stands upon the Mole, when we swept into the harbor and came to anchor amid a vast crowd of ships, steamers and small coasting vessels. It was a magnificent scene which burst upon our vision. *Genoa la Superba!* Genoa, the city of palaces, the ancient empress of the sea, whose merchants were princes, and her princes merchants, lay before us. A vast amphitheatre of hills, crowned with tasteful villas, with splendid palaces, with glorious temples, with solid ramparts, and with hanging gardens and terraces, where the orange and the lime flourish, rises directly from the sea, while beyond it the glorious Appenines, in all their wondrous grandeur, lift their heads towards the clouds, and make up a scene of unsurpassed magnificence. Making our way to the shore, through a throng of vessels, we find ourselves well-provided for in one of the ancient palaces, now transformed into a hotel.

To describe Genoa is but to repeat what has already been said of Naples, Rome and Florence. We pass through the same endless succession of churches and palaces, and see the same evidences of Italian genius and taste. Most of the streets are exceedingly narrow, many of the great thoroughfares of business being only from eight to ten feet wide, and some are not more than six. These are built up with houses six and eight stories high, and are so crooked and intricate that a stranger can most readily lose his way in them. As you ascend the heights, however, they become more spacious, and present to your admiring gaze long series of marble palaces, which have for generations been the homes of the princes of Genoa.

One of the peculiar features of the city is the graceful and beautiful attire of the ladies, who universally wear a veil thrown over their heads, fastened with pins to their glossy hair, and then flowing over their shoulders to the waist. When the most fashionable portion of the female population appear in public with these veils gathered in graceful folds over their black hair, and daintily held in place by their taper fingers, they have a most charming and picturesque appearance which one cannot but admire.

The heights around Genoa afford many rich and magnificent views. You stand in the midst of a vast and glorious panorama of hill and mountain, valley and city, while at your feet are the countless palaces, villas and cathedrals, which have won for Genoa the title of the Superb. But we cannot linger here. Far away to the north stand the snow-clad Alps, forming an eternal barrier between Italy, France and Switzerland, and they are inviting us to their cool retreats and their glorious altars, which have been built without hands, as the fitting ornaments for the temple which God has made for Himself—a temple whose shining arch is the bright heaven, and whose choral music is the murmur of the winds, the voice of the waters, and the roar of the avalanche.

Taking the cars at Genoa, we are whirled away over the plains of Sardinia, where every step gives us the assurance that the country is governed by a man whose liberal and extended views are leading him to seek the highest welfare of his people. We reach Turin at night, and, taking the omnibus of the *Hôtel de le Bretagne*, ride through broad and beautiful streets, well paved and brilliantly illuminated, to the very heart of the city, near the ancient castle, still surrounded by its deep moat, but now used as the General Police Office of Piedmont. Turin contains about 125,000 inhabitants, and has every appearance of prosperity. It is built on an extended plain, upon the northern side of the Po, which is crossed by several fine bridges. It contains over one hundred churches, many of which are remarkable for their decorations and the splendor of their architecture. The royal palace is one of the finest in Europe, and, besides its splendid paintings and statuary, presents the most perfect arrangements for domestic comfort and enjoyment. As the King was absent, we were permitted to visit the private rooms of the royal family, which are fitted up with the most exquisite taste, and appear to have been designed to give to the royal inmates everything which art and taste can yield to make for them a pleasant home.

One of the marked features of Turin are the vast colonnades, which make the side-walks a pleasant resort, either in the heat of summer, or the rains and storms of winter. Here, beneath these long arches, extending from the river to the castle, and branching off thence into streets which are built upon the same plan, are the great marts of Piedmont, filled with every article of traffic, and crowded with citizens or peasants, with their quaint and antique dresses, who have come from the country to exchange their produce for the luxuries which the city affords. The streets of Turin present the usual contrasts of Italian towns, although the amount of beggary here is sensibly diminished. It is doubtless the best built city in Europe. The erection of its buildings is not left to private taste and caprice, but is committed to an officer, whose assent must be gained before a single house can be erected. As a result of this, the whole town is uniform, and the dwellings are substantially built. Nothing but such an arrangement could ever have produced that splendid arcade, of which I have just spoken. Here and there, throughout the city, are pleasant squares or piazzas, which add not only to its beauty, but are also greatly promotive of its health.

The walks and drives around Turin are of great beauty. Crossing the Po by its magnificent bridge of marble and granite, we come to a range of hills upon which stand several churches and buildings, presenting, from their elevation, a most picturesque appearance. As we look across the plain, westward and northward, the whole gigantic chain of the Alps is before us, shadowing away in the distance, but, nearer at hand, shining in the brilliant light which is for ever reflected from their eternal snows. Here, at the foot of these stupendous mountains, is the home of the early witnesses of the Truth; and towards that spot we turn, with all the ardor of the pilgrim who has travelled long and far to stand amid the scenes and struggles and triumphs of the Israel of the Alps. Taking the cars at the western suburb of Turin, we ride, for an hour and a half, through a beautiful country, well cultivated, and pleasantly diversified with plain and hill and gentle streams, and luxuriant with olives, figs and the mulberry. Twenty miles from Turin is Pignerolo, the terminus of the railroad, lying upon hills which command most extensive views. The approach to the city, as it rises upon this noble amphitheatre, is strikingly beautiful. For several miles the main avenue is lined with luxuriant vines, running from tree to tree. From the summit of a gently swelling hill, a picturesque convent peeps out from the midst of fig-trees and vineyards, while upon a terrace, which overlooks the vast plains of Piedmont, stands a lofty and imposing cathedral.

On landing at the station we found that the diligence had already started for La Tour, and that the next stage would not leave until evening. After looking over the city, with its many sad symptoms of decay, and at the hotel, the appearance of which was by no means inviting, we determined to charter a carriage to carry us to La Tour, some seven miles distant. We should hesitate some time before using such a conveyance in this city, for such a turn-out is not witnessed every day, either as regards horse, carriage, or postilion. But it safely conveyed us through a country growing every moment more and more interesting, until the valleys of

Piedmont were reached, and, crossing a foaming torrent which came down from the Alpine snows, we entered the capital of the Waldensian valleys. It was a most grateful relief to find ourselves away from the pomp and magnificence upon which we had so long been gazing, and resting amid the quiet beauty of this hallowed spot. It was a pleasant contrast to the heat and dust of the city, which we found in these glorious hills that rose above us. Nor was the utter contrast to all we had seen in Italy complete until we entered our chamber at the hotel, and found on our table a copy of the Testament in French and German—the first, except our own Bible, which we had met with in Italy. It was a token that we were passing out of the terrible shadows of priestly traditions into the blessed sunlight of the Word of God.

The Waldensian territory embraces a space twenty-three by eighteen miles, having, in the mutations of centuries, been greatly reduced from its original limits. It lies upon the southeastern slope of that vast range of mountains which divides Italy from France and Savoy.

Its shape is triangular, taking the ridges of the Alps for its base. Here, among one of the wildest scenes of Nature, nestle the smiling valleys of Piedmont, the homes of the ancient Church of God, the witnesses for His truth through long ages of corruption and darkness. La Tour, the capital, lies within the valley of Luzerne. Just at the entrance to the village is a Roman Catholic church, around which are the usual amount of beggars; beyond stretches a long and crooked street, with no pretensions whatever to architectural beauties, filled with comfortable houses, built with stone, and most of them roofed with the same material. Towards the other extremity of the village is the beautiful church, erected by contributions from England and America. Near by, surrounded by a pleasant green, is the College, a plain, substantial edifice; beyond which are the residences of the professors, built after the plainest possible models, and in perfect keeping with the primitive simplicity which everywhere prevails. In the rear of the village a mountain torrent goes thundering down, to add its waters to the

Po. On either hand rise the steep spurs of the Alpine range, far up whose sides are the stone cottages of the Waldenses. The scenery throughout this valley is of the wildest and most imposing character. As you advance upwards from La Tour, the mountains close in on either hand, until the valleys become mere wild ravines; yet, in the most rugged portions of them may be seen little patches of grain and grass, in the midst of which the peasant has made his home. Nothing can exceed in beauty and romance the scenes which now open, with some new and fresh interest at every turn. Far above you rise the hoary mountains, placed there like watchful sentinels to guard the repose of the simple-hearted people whose homes they shelter. Wild and narrow defiles—foaming torrents rushing down their mountain beds—peaceful lakelets, embosomed in the hills, and reflecting, like polished mirrors, the outlines of nature—and meadows of unrivalled beauty and fertility, form a contrast of awful grandeur, and attractive loveliness and grace. Here is the spot where Christianity found a home amid the early persecutions of the church, confirming the Apocalyptic vision of the woman fleeing into the wilderness to escape the dragon which sought to destroy herself and her child.

There are five valleys lying between these stupendous ranges of hills, mainly converging at La Tour, and containing a population of about 22,000, of whom a few are Roman Catholics, who, under the present mild and paternal government of Sardinia, are prevented from manifesting that ancient hatred which for ages made this country the scene of sore and bitter persecutions. I found that Dr. Revel, the moderator of the Waldensian Synod, (to whom I had letters,) was absent at Milan, but through the kindness of his excellent wife I was introduced to several of the professors, and to Mr. Charbonnier, the acting pastor of La Tour. The morning after my arrival was the Sabbath, the day of all others which I wished to spend in these valleys. At an early hour I walked with Prof. Thon up to the old church of the Copiès, one of the two which were left standing when the Vaudois returned from their banishment by the

Papal authorities. Leaving the streets of the village, and following the course of a beautiful stream which comes winding down from the hills, we ascend towards those gigantic mountains, whose peaks stand out in clear and well defined outlines against the sky. Almost above us, upon our right, is the bold rock of Castelluzzo, memorable during the persecutions of the Waldenses as a natural fortress, to whose summit mothers and children were borne, to find refuge from the assaults of their merciless enemies, and from which many were thrown down and perished. Across the valley rises another Alpine spur, cultivated almost to its summit, while before us loom up distant peaks, where clouds and storm make their home, and amid whose awful solitudes the eagle builds her nest.

It was a most interesting sight to see all the avenues and paths leading to the church, filled with peasants on their way to the place of worship. Venerable patriarchs, with their children and their children's children, were walking towards the house of God. Matrons with their daughters, simply and neatly attired, and with their unique head-dresses, were descending the various mountain paths. Strong men and youth were clambering up some romantic gorge, all moved by one impulse,—to worship the God of their fathers. As they met each other, pleasant salutations were exchanged, and to us the hat was respectfully lifted, as they recognized in us strangers from a distant land.

The old church is built of stone, and in its entire absence of all ornament offers a strange contrast to the splendid temples which we had everywhere seen in Italy. But never, by all the pompous services we had seen elsewhere, were we so moved as by the simple scene which there presented itself. Yes, that venerable church, with no altars; with no splendid statuary or paintings; with no throngs of robed priests and mitred prelates; with no chant swelling up amid the light that comes streaming through stained glass and gothic windows; with no organ peals resounding through lofty arches, and filling the vast space with glorious music—yet surpassed all I had yet visited, in its thrilling associations.

What is St. Peter's when contrasted with this

gigantic temple, built without hands, which for ages has sheltered the Church of Christ? What were all its pompous services to the simple, devout, and pious utterances of a people, the successors of a line of Christians whose history goes back to the early dawn of Christianity upon the Italian mountains?

As I entered the humble sanctuary, I took a seat near the pulpit and looked over the large audience, and I could not but remark the entire contrast which was presented, to the pomp, pageantry, and childish follies upon which I had been looking for the past month. The people were evidently peasants in the most humble circumstances. As they entered the church, each one stood for a moment in a reverent attitude, evidently uttering a silent prayer. The women were seated upon one side of the church, and the men upon the other. The service began with a lesson from God's Word, read by the teacher who sits below the pulpit, and who also acts the part of a precentor. At the reading of the Law, the congregation all rise; after which the minister, dressed in a simple robe, makes, on behalf of the people, a general confession of sin. The prayers are brief but comprehensive, and are mostly read from a published form. The music is congregational, and at present consists in singing the Psalms, without any attempt at rythm or versification. The sermon, by Mr. Charbonnier, was, at the first service, a simple exposition of a portion of Scripture, designed mainly for the instruction of the catechumens, or youth who are undergoing a course of preparation for the communion.

At ten o'clock, a second service was held in the church at La Tour, a large and pleasant edifice, well filled with a serious and attentive audience. A group of nearly 300 children were gathered there in the afternoon, and it was delightful to see the interest which they manifested in the duties of the hour, the readiness with which they gave scriptural answers to the questions proposed, and the happy faculty which their pastor possessed of enlisting and retaining their attention. In the evening a service was held with the children at the Orphan Asylum, which consisted of some simple devotional exercises, and a brief exposition of a passage of the Word of God. At the close of the meeting, I begged the teacher to let them sing for me one song—"*La Belle Patrie*," (There is a Happy Land)—and so they gathered around the door in the open air, and sang it as I have often heard it in my own beloved Sabbath-school at home. As those sweet tones died away, I could not help trying to say a few words to that little group, and to tell them that I had come from America to see their people, and that my sincere wish for them was, that they might love the Saviour, who took little children in His arms, and would at last receive all who trust Him, in that "Happy Land" where there would be no sin nor sorrow.

The history of the Waldenses must ever excite the deepest sympathy and interest of all who love the Church of God. They were for ages the witnesses for His truth, and kept alive a pure and evangelical religion, when all the world had gone after the lying wonders of the Man of Sin. Their written history does not go back beyond the tenth or eleventh century; but their traditions indicate that there was a church amid these mountain fastnesses ages before, and that during the times of persecutions, the people of God here found a refuge in the wilderness. As the Italian Church began to feel the growing tendencies to corruption in the increase of priestly power and splendor, this simple people remained unaffected thereby, and kept alive the early doctrines and institutions of Christianity. Shut up in their mountain homes, they were satisfied with the simplicity of the gospel, and desired none of those regal forms and splendid ceremonies which were taking the place of the truth and the original ordinances of Christ.

Their early confessions, and especially the "Noble Lesson," show that their creed has ever been evangelical and pure. How the Romish Church, in its hatred of the gospel, has fearfully and bitterly persecuted this people, is well known. The history of their expulsion from the valleys and their final return, is familiar to all. At the Reformation they sent two delegates to have an interview with the Reformers, and when they heard what was their design and their creed, they gave them a hearty "God Speed!" and the right hand of fellowship.

Their form of church government resembles that of the Continental Protestant churches, being essentially Presbyterian. There are about sixteen congregations in the valleys, each of them being governed by a Consistory composed of the pastor and elders, who are represented and united in a Synod, corresponding to the Presbytery and Classis of the Scotch and Dutch churches. The executive of the Synod is a Table, or Committee of ministers and laymen, of which body Dr. Revel is the present Moderator, having been recently reäppointed by the Synod.

The Waldensian church evidently has for its special work the evangelization of Italy. Already a number of missions have been established, and churches built at several important points, and the Truth is making its way with evident success.

The present King of Sardinia, though himself a Roman Catholic, gives ample protection to the Vaudois, although they are not left without evidences of the bitter hatred which the

Papal priesthood cherishes towards them, and of the jealousy with which their movements are regarded. Yet the restrictions which were once laid upon them are greatly mitigated, and the heavy penalties, which prevented any effort for the evangelization of Italy, are almost entirely removed.

The Vaudois are in every respect a wonderful people. Though mostly poor, no beggars are seen among them. The peasants live high up among the mountains, cultivating every available spot of ground, and living in the most simple and frugal style. Although depending mostly upon foreign benefactions for the support of their ministry and educational institutions, they yet give of their poverty for the missionary work, and regard themselves as especially designed of Providence to spread the truth in Italy. For this purpose they have established a college, in which about 100 youth are receiving an education, and have, mainly through the benevolence of American Christians, endowed a theological faculty for the purpose of fitting young men for the ministry.

The college stands at the entrance to the valley, looking out upon the mountains which have been for ages the retreat of the Church of God, and the shelter of His persecuted people. In yonder Roman Catholic village stands the old nunnery which tradition connects with many a tale of persecution and death. Every hill has a voice and a story, and tells of fearful trials endured for a testimony to the truth. Here, amid these scenes and memories, the Vaudois youth can prepare for the work of the ministry, and, stimulated by the wonderful history of their people, can quietly pass through the necessary preparations for the duties before them, and fit themselves to carry forth the truth which their fathers loved, and for which many yielded up their lives. From this spot they will go forth to meet the coming wants of Italy; and, as the people, tired and disgusted with the mummeries of Popery, shall desire to know the truth as it is in Jesus, they will hear it from the lips of a ministry which is truly Apostolic, and from a Church which has never been "reformed," because never corrupted.

X.

THE ALPS.

IT was a day of intense heat in which we bade adieu to Turin and to Italy, and turned our faces towards those glorious Alpine peaks which, in solemn grandeur, rose before us. The usual annoyances of *visas* to our passports were to be undergone; the Swiss consul was to be consulted, and his consent to our passage into Switzerland obtained; permission of the police was to be had for our leaving Turin, and then places were to be secured in the cars and diligence for Geneva. It was no small tax upon our patience, after attending to all these preliminaries, to await the time of the officials at the station; to have every article of baggage weighed, marked, and taxed, and then for almost an hour to look for the return of the omnibus which was to convey us to the railway. We were not sorry for any little by-play to occupy our thoughts, and we watched, with uncommon interest, the movements of a party of street-acrobats, who, laying down a carpet and spring-board, performed sundry grotesque gymnastic feats. As chairs were very scarce, my friend Rogers and myself improvised seats for the ladies of our party from piles of port-manteaus, carpet-bags, and shawls, while he and I stretched ourselves upon the pavement, presenting quite an oriental appearance to the passers-by, and, on the whole, taking matters pretty much at our ease. Just as the omnibus arrived for its load, one of our party, from Rome—the lady with six immense travelling-trunks—drove up with her courier, having decided to honor us with her company over the Alps. For a time there appeared to be every prospect that the cars would be half-way to Susa before our load should arrive at the station; but with the aid of porters and officers, and amid a great many not very elegant Italian oaths, we were finally disposed of, lady and all, and arrived in time to secure our places.

The cars on this road are exceedingly comfortable, and our way led through a country which grew every moment more wild and interesting. On the one hand was the foaming torrent of the Dora, fed by the snows of the Alps, rushing down to join the Po at Turin, and then to become a highway for commerce, and to flow by fifty cities ere it reached the Mediterranean. On the other hand were mountains, pressing more and more upon the road, until at Susa they made further progress by rail impracticable,—and we came to the foot of Mount Cenis, through whose wild passes we were to find our way to Switzerland.

Here we found a large encampment of French soldiers—their white tents shining in the clear light of the full moon, which was riding gloriously through the heavens and giving almost the distinctness of day to every object around us. As the cars arrive, everything around the station is full of life and bustle. Three large diligences are awaiting their loads of passengers and baggage; conductors and agents are reading off the names of the passengers, and assigning to each one his proper place; hungry people are running into the refreshment rooms to lay in a supply for the night's travel; others are arranging their overcoats and shawls for use in the anticipated cold of the mountain passes; long ladders are placed to the top of the diligences, upon which men are busily engaged in packing away huge piles of trunks, among which are the small Saratoga *houses* of our lady fellow-traveller, and about which she is giving her courier a most sound rating—for she well knew how to scold: name after name is called off, to which some person answers, steps out, and takes the place assigned him by the conductor. Three of us mount to the *banquette*, the only place which could be obtained for love or money, and which is, after all, *the* place in a diligence for mountain travel. And perhaps I had better pause here, to describe a diligence. It is a huge, lumbering vehicle, containing some four or five compartments. The *coupé*, the most aristocratic and high-priced, which will hold three or four persons, is in the front; the *interieur*, which will contain some seven or eight passengers, is back of this; the *rotonde* is in the rear, and the *banquette*, which is generally considered the worst of the four, is above the *coupé*. We took the *banquette*, for it was Hobson's choice with us—either that or nothing.

Twelve mules are attached to this vast machine, with its ship-load of passengers and baggage; the conductor ascends to our side, where he can direct the whole and manage the brakes; two postilions, in their monkey-jackets, mount upon their saddles, and with a shout and crack of the whip, the word, "*en route, postillon,*" is given, and we begin the ascent of the Alps. There is an air of romance about a diligence ride up these mountains which makes it exceedingly attractive. The wild songs and shouts of the postilions, with the incessant accompaniment of the crack of the whip, as they urge their mules along these steep acclivities; the loud roar of the Alpine torrent as it rolls and thunders by; the excitement which attends the passage of some tremendous abyss, which shrinks away from your feet into almost unfathomable depths, while on the other side a mountain spur, with its sharp and bold outlines, stands up like a giant to dispute your progress; the intense delight with which some new and majestic feature of the mountains is welcomed; the solemn and awful grandeur of these mighty hills that rise up to the clouds, all combine to give to the traveller a pleasure that no work of art could ever produce. These are the solemn altars of the temple which was built without hands, and whose choral echo is the universe.

Occasionally a train of baggage passes us, or small, straggling companies of soldiers; or a muleteer, with his load, goes singing and shouting by. Here and there a small hamlet indicates the existence of hardy mountaineers, who are improving the last foothold of vegetable life; or a hospice or hostelry is planted by the roadside, for the assistance of wayworn and weary travellers.

I cannot forget, though I cannot well express, the emotions I felt when, on awaking from a short sleep, just in the grey of the morning, I looked upward and saw, high above us, the lofty peaks of the Alps, covered with perpetual snows. The cold had now so increased that every shawl and overcoat was in demand, although it was the middle of the month of July. The air was sharp and clear, and, as the day dawned, the scene which opened before us was one of awful grandeur. On every hand rose high and rugged peaks, gleaming in the light of the morning sun. Here and there, vast gullies, cut in the mountain-side, marked the track of an avalanche; while upon the hill-side of the road were occasional excavations made as places of safety when the rocks and snows of the mountain are making their annual descent to the valley. Near the summit of Mount Cenis, six thousand eight hundred and twenty-five feet above the sea, stands an old hospice, originally founded by Charlemagne, in the ninth century, when crossing this pass with his army. The present edifice was built by Napoleon I., a part of which is occupied by a corps of soldiers, and the rest by Benedictine monks, who reside here that they may aid the weary and benighted traveller.

At this point the scenery is sublime. Deep valleys, and fearful ravines, through which wild mountain torrents are foaming, spring away from our side, down to almost interminable depths. The beautiful scenery of Italy has been exchanged for the wild and rugged grandeur of the mountains. The olive and the vine have long since disappeared. Here and there are small patches of grass, amid which stands the *châlet* of the mountaineer, where his cows are grazing, while still higher his goats are cropping the herbage which forces its way up between the rocks. The road, as it winds by these tremendous ravines, with its zigzag course, often lies upon the very verge, so that the brain almost whirls as we look down and think what would be the result of a single mistake in directing the diligence, or of the slightest accident to our ponderous vehicle. Along the way there are built, at intervals, Houses of Refuge, where live the *cantonniers*, who are engaged in mending the road and in aiding the needy. From the post, on the summit of Mt. Cenis, to Lans-Le-Bourg, the peasants use sledges, in the winter, when the snow has filled up the ravines, and by this means they descend the mountain in about ten minutes, passing over a distance that requires from two to three hours to ascend.

As we pass downward, through scenes of the grandest and wildest character, we find, high above one of the gorges, a strong and well-built fortress, whose batteries command the passage to Italy. A beautiful bridge, hanging high in the air, and connecting the fort with the road, has the expressive name of the *Pont du Diable*, or the Devil's Bridge. Lans-Le-Bourg, at the foot of Mt. Cenis, is the first Swiss town with which we meet. It is a long, straggling village, with only one principal street, exceedingly narrow and filthy, and filled with numerous *cabarets*, which furnish a breakfast of coffee, hard bread, and a pipe of tobacco. As the road winds down from this point—which, although at the foot of the mountain, is four thousand four hundred feet above the sea level—it opens upon a most beautiful and romantic gorge, in which lies the valley of St. Michael, where commences the tunnel under the Alps, which is to connect France and Italy by a passage nine miles long.

At St. Jean de Maurienne we leave the lumbering diligence, and are hurried by cars through beautiful scenes, by lakes and rivers, cataracts, mountains, plains, and valleys, until we arrive at the city of Geneva, situated upon the lake whose name it bears. This city, containing about 32,000 inhabitants, stands just at the foot of the lake, where the blue waters of the arrowy Rhone sweep toward the valleys of France. A substantial bridge connects the two portions of the city, which lies upon the slope of two hills, divided by the Rhone. As seen from the lake, Geneva presents an exceedingly beautiful appearance. Along the banks is a fine street or quay, and a beautiful public garden has been laid out, and forms an exceedingly desirable promenade on a warm evening. The city is divided into lower and upper towns, somewhat like Edinburgh. Standing at the window of our hotel, we have a view far up the lake, dotted here and there with the white lateen sails of passing vessels. In the distance is the noble range of the Jura mountains, stretching away to the south and west. If we walk across the bridge at sunset, we have a splendid view of the Mont Blanc range, amid which the hoary monarch of the mountains lifts his awful head to the clouds. It is amid these two ranges that Byron lays the scene of the storm which he has so wonderfully and graphically described:

> . . . . . Far along,
> From peak to peak the rattling crags among,
> Leaps the live thunder! Not from one lone cloud,
> But every mountain now has found a tongue,
> And Jura answers, through her misty shroud,
> Back to the joyous Alps, who call to her aloud!

The city of Geneva owes its chief interest to its having been the home of Calvin. Here, when leaving France, he was met by the Reformers, who compelled him to remain among them. Here he wrote his great theological works, and accomplished an amount of varied labor which broke down his health at an early age. The old cathedral of St. Peter's, the edifice in which he preached, is still in the possession of the established church, and a portion of the pulpit is pointed out as the old desk at which he uttered the glorious truths of the gospel. His grave has nothing to distinguish it, save a stone with the initials J. C.

One of the pleasantest excursions from Geneva is a sail down the beautiful lake upon which the city stands. It is about forty miles long, lying 1142 feet above the sea level, and is of most exquisite beauty, its scenery possessing the charms of almost endless variety. As the steamer turns upwards from Geneva, the magnificent summits of Mt. Blanc, fifty miles distant, are distinctly seen, while along the shores of the lake are lovely villas, picturesque churches, and thriving towns and watering-places. Near the end of the lake stands the castle of Chillon, an old feudal fortress, whose interior presents a fine idea of the rough and rugged times in which it was built. Here is laid the scene of Byron's " Prisoner of Chillon." The castle stands upon an isolated rock, and was built in the year 1238, as a State Prison. Here, for six years, Bonnivard, who had sought the freedom of Geneva, was confined in a dungeon just at the level of the lake. The ring to which he was chained is still there. Near by, the beam which once served as a gallows for the condemned prisoners is seen, while, in another part of the castle, is a small staircase, which terminates in a fearful well, eighty feet deep, down which many a victim was hurled, and so disappeared from the world forever. No wonder that the poet writes of this spot:

> "Chillon! thy prison is an holy place,
> And thy sad floor an altar, for 'twas trod
> Until his very steps had left a trace
> Worn, as if the cold pavement were a sod,
> By Bonnivard: may none these marks efface,
> For they appeal from tyranny to God."

Early in the week the diligence, in which our places had been taken several days before, drove out of the city of Geneva for the vale of Chamouny, fifty miles distant. Our route lay through an exceedingly picturesque country. At the town of Anemasse we enter Savoy, where our passports are examined, and the baggage taken down and inspected. As we continue to ascend, unmistakable evidences of our approach to the Alpine regions abound. The stream that rushes by us becomes more turbulent and rapid, and the worn and whitened rocks show traces of the winter's flood, and are an indisputable proof of its power. As we advance toward the mountains, the scenery becomes more wild and awful. Huge precipices frown above us, and at our feet lie vast and dark ravines. Bold mountain peaks stand up in clear relief against the sky. Vast rugged rocks lie in the deep defiles, whither they have fallen from their native ledges in the hills above. At Sallenche we pause for dinner, which we prefer to eat under the porch of the hotel, that we may enjoy, uninterruptedly, the magnificent scene which now opens to view. Just across the river is a noble range of precipitous hills, rising into huge cliffs, which are called "needles," affording a beautiful contrast to the Forclaz, with its sides covered with pines and its top with pasturage. At our feet lies a deep gorge, while above and beyond all, Mont Blanc, still twelve miles distant, but appearing near at hand, lifts its majestic head above the clouds, and shines in the splendor of an unclouded day. Yet even here, amid these glorious creations of the Almighty, one is compelled to witness poverty and degradation. Crowds of beggars surround the hotel, and follow the carriage, nearly all of them afflicted with that shocking disease of the Alps, the goitre, and many of them being idiots of the very lowest character. The goitre is a large excrescence upon the neck, and it is more frequent with women than with men. Although a horrible deformity, it is said to be attended with no pain. This disease is very common in the Alps. But even these sufferers are nothing to the Cretins. The Cretin is a vacant and hopeless idiot, whose huge head, shrivelled limbs, inarticulate words, distorted features, meaningless face, and staring eyes, present a spectacle which, once seen, can never be forgotten. I shall never forget two whom I saw, father and son. The son was blind, deaf, and dumb, and just able to stand, and both were in the most horrid and abject poverty.

At Sallenche the diligence is exchanged for a *char-à-banc.* This vehicle is simply an old, rickety, broken-down, rheumatic and most uncomfortable two-horse carriage. In our case it was rendered still more uncomfortable by the presence of a very queer sort of passenger, who occupied the fourth seat, and whose room would have been infinitely preferable to his company. He made all sorts of strange antics, and put himself in most uncouth positions, winding up by sitting on the top of the carriage and dangling his feet in our faces, and this while the vehicle was on the edge of the precipice, leaning over it until one almost anticipated a headlong fall. The ride from Sallenche to Chamouny is about fourteen miles by measurement, although it is, probably, fifty miles in feeling. But the scenery well repays us for the fatigue. Some magnificent views may be obtained by leaving the carriage and turning a little aside from the main path. One of these is peculiarly grand. From a slight elevation above the road, the eye takes in a magnificent panorama, presenting an Alpine scene of indescribable wildness and rugged grandeur. Down a dark and awful gorge, filled with vast masses of rock, which have been gathering there for ages, roll the foaming waters of the Arve, bearing down with it the fine sand which has been worn away from the Alps by the action of the glaciers upon them. Beyond this rise huge and rocky peaks, desolate and barren, blackened by the storms of centuries. Far away in the distance are smiling valleys and plains, while here and there around us are the rude châlets of the hardy Savoyards, and groups of peasants, busy in gathering in their mountain harvest of grain and grass; while children are busy turning the new-mown hay, and women are bearing it home upon their heads in huge bundles.

Towards the close of the day we ascend the last hill which lies between us and Chamouny, and, coming to a sudden turn of the road, see at one glance the beautiful valley, with the vast glaciers which lie down upon its very verge, mingling the snows and ice of winter with the luxuriance of summer. The spot where we are standing is called the Montets, a steep and stony ascent, from which we obtain fine views of the enormous peak of Mont Blanc. As we pass the glaciers which come down to the valley, we observe the furious torrents which descend from them, and which are formed by the constant melting of the ice in the intense heat of the sun. The village of Chamouny, which lies in the valley, is a collection of Swiss châlets, cottages, and fine hotels, with the ordinary bustle of a watering-place. It is surrounded by the vast ranges of the Alps, which spring up on either hand, leaving between them only a narrow strip of land susceptible of cultivation, and affording many very good spots for farming purposes. The river Arve flows through it, and even here, within a few miles of its source, is a wild, deep and furious stream.

I need not say how sweet was the sleep which followed a fatiguing ride of fifty miles, with long, toilsome walks up steep hills, where walking even was some relief to the miseries of a wretched *char-à-banc*. But with the early dawn I was awake and astir to obtain my first daylight view of Mont Blanc. I was at length in that spot which had formed the subject of many a delicious reverie. In all my thoughts of Europe, Chamouny was a word which called up scenes and visions of beauty which I knew must abundantly repay the toil with which the valley was to be visited; and now, as I looked around, I felt that, truly, the half had not been told.

What were all the palaces and works of art to the scene which now burst upon our sight? What were all the temples of Italy to this gorgeous temple, built by Him who setteth fast the mountains?

> "Above me are the Alps,
> The palaces of Nature, whose vast walls
> Have pinnacled in cloud their snowy scalps,
> And throned Eternity in icy halls
> Of cold sublimity, where forms and falls
> The avalanche, the thunderbolt of snow!
> All that expands the spirit, yet appalls,
> Gathers around these summits, as to show
> How Earth may pierce to Heaven, and leave vain man below."

I took a position whence I could see the awful summit of Mont Blanc rising above the sea to the height of 15,760 feet! As the day dawned, its first faint light rested upon the top of this monarch of the mountains. Gradually the shadows which were yet lying upon the hills and valleys disappeared, bringing more and more distinctly into view the outlines of the magnificent panorama which lay around us. At length one bright ray of sunlight rested upon the head of Mont Blanc, and then other points were rapidly illuminated, and their long shadows fell upon the more distant summits, until at length every peak was gleaming in the morning light, and day broke upon the mountains. That sight, which I had so long anticipated, I shall not soon forget. Its wondrous beauty will be a "joy forever."

As I stood gazing upon it, the words of Coleridge, written in the vale of Chamouny, and which, from boyhood, had made me desirous to look upon these scenes, were recalled with all their power and beauty, as a fit utterance of the emotions which were swelling within me.

> "Hast thou a charm to stay the morning star
> In his steep course, so long he seems to pause
> On thy bald, awful head, O ' sovran Blanc?'
> O dread and silent mount, I gazed upon thee
> 'Till thou, still present to the bodily sense,
> Didst vanish from my thoughts—entranced in prayer
> I worshipped the Invisible alone.
>
> "Thou, too, hoar Mount! with thy sky-pointing peaks,
> Rose like a cloud of incense from the earth!
> Thou kingly Spirit, throned among the hills!

> Thou dread Ambassador from Earth to Heaven!
> Great Hierarch! tell thou the silent sky,
> And tell the stars, and tell yon rising sun,
> Earth, with her thousand voices, praises God!"

From this glorious scene I turned away, to make preparations for an excursion to the *Mer de Glace*. After an early breakfast, our mules were at the door, and we set off in the saddle with two excellent guides. Crossing the roaring river by a substantial bridge, and shortly after the Avernon, by a more primitive structure, we soon began to ascend an almost precipitous mountain by a small mule-pass cut in its side, and which winds up by a zigzag route, across the tracks of avalanches, amid huge and ragged rocks, by the rustic châlets of the mountaineers, and often on the very verge of tremendous ravines and precipices that start away from our feet, and almost make the head dizzy with the sight of their fearful depths. After a ride of about three hours we reach an elevation of over five thousand feet, and turning around the angle of a rustic hostelry, our enthusiastic guides shout, "*Voila la Mer de Glace!*" and the wondrous scene is before us. This glacier lies in one of the valleys of Mont Blanc, and is fed by the eternal snows upon its summit. It is about twelve miles long by from half a mile to a mile and a half broad, and the ice, broken up into thousands of hummocks, and opening as many fearful chasms, is supposed to be from two to seven hundred feet thick. As it proceeds downward with a daily motion of about fourteen inches, it carries with it the rocks of the mountain, which are ground to powder in the passage, and are carried away by the waters of the Avernon, which issue from a dark cavern at the foot of the glacier. Far up on either side are sharp and bold peaks of rock, called *aiguilles*, or needles, which form a decided and beautiful feature of this whole Alpine range, and which are a glorious fringe to this majestic sea of ice. There are many points from which this scene is surveyed by tourists, each of which presents some new attraction. All should descend from Montanvert by the precipitous path which leads to the glacier, that they may walk upon it, and stand upon the verge of those fearful gulfs, formed by the downward motion of the ice.

Such are the changes made upon the surface of the glacier by its motion, that a new path across the icy sea has to be marked out every morning. The progress of the sea is indicated by masses of rocks which have fallen upon it from the precipices above, and which are moving downward to join the vast piles of *débris* accumulated into hills in the valley below. In regard to the width of this glacier I do not speak positively. The air is so clear, and the surrounding objects are so unusual, that it is almost impossible to judge correctly of distances. It takes forty-five minutes to cross, however. There are flags along the route to direct the guides, but even then we sometimes get between two ravines which are closing together, and are forced to retrace our steps.

But we must not linger here. Returning to our hotel by the same zigzag route, the descent of which is more dangerous than the ascent, we may spend a pleasant afternoon in the valley, amid the bazaars for the sale of Swiss woodwork, much of which is of an exceedingly beautiful character. Early on the following morning we are again in the saddle, with our carpet-bags and shawls strapped on behind us, and, passing through the beautiful valley of Chamouny, from which we obtain an upward view of several fine glaciers, we leave its romantic hamlets and villages, and, journeying toward the passes which lead to Martigny and the valley of the Rhone, begin the ascent of the Col de Balme. Thirty long and weary miles are to be passed over,—but the day is fine, the air bracing, the guides attentive, and the scenery is beautiful. Toiling up the steep sides of the mountain we soon leave all vegetation behind us, except the few hardy shrubs and grasses that can endure the long and severe winters. Here and there a peasant is looking after some cows, or goats climbing up the dizzy precipices to the green spots warmed into beauty by the summer's sun. It is the middle of July, but the snow is still lying here and there around us, and a thousand little streams are laughing their way down to the valley. I made a capital snow-ball, when stopping for dinner at the little hostelry on the summit of the mountain, where we arrived after a ride of about five hours. At this point, 7,550 feet from the sea, Mont Blanc appears before us in all its vast proportions, soaring above all the surrounding peaks, shining cold, clear and bright against the cloudless sky. Resuming our journey, after a plain dinner of bread and milk, we descend to the valley of the Trient, cross a rapid stream, leave the romantic hamlet, composed of rude châlets, and pass onward, through pine forests, with here and there a green patch, or meadow, or field of barley, on our way towards the Forclaz. Here our passports are examined, at a lonely police station, new *visas* impressed upon it, and we begin our descent towards the valley of the Rhone, winding down a zigzag path, with short and abrupt turns, which sometimes bring either the heads or tails of our mules over a precipice, down which we may cast a stone that shall fall a thousand feet before it touches the earth, to rebound down the dark ravines which shrink away at our feet. It is a wild and fearful path, but the views of the valley are magnificent, and well repay the toil.

11*

As we advance, signs of civilization appear, and increase at every step. Peasant girls, with baskets of cherries, and other fruits, are offering us their articles of traffic; beggars are soliciting alms; farmers are gathering in their crops; women and children are turning over the new-mown hay, and large and well-laden wagons are slowly passing with their loads of grain. We are a most sorry party when we arrive at Martigny, and could not have proceeded much further if we had tried. Resuming our journey by rail and steamer, we pass the beautiful falls of the Pissevache; an old hermitage, perched high upon a precipice; lonely valleys and villages; through Lausanne, the lake Neuchatel and Bienne, to the quaint city of Bern, and at last arrive at the most charming and attractive of all the places of Switzerland—Interlaken. I can see that delightful valley now. The guide-books say, that if you lose a friend on the road, you'll be sure to find him there. Ladies are generally taken sick there, and say to their husbands, "Do you journey on by yourselves and see all that is to be seen. We are too tired to go further. Don't be gone *more* than a month, and we'll wait for you here at Interlaken." Truly, it is the best place in Europe for a summer's enjoyment, and I do not see that I could do better than leave you there for a week, and meet you again, to journey with you down the Rhine.

XI.

THE RHINE.

THE omnibus, loaded within and without, set us down, by our direction, at the Pension Ritschard (at Interlaken) which in Murray's account of that place has this brief but decided notice: "Quiet and comfortable." A pleasant experience of several days at that hotel, enables us to give our full and free endorsement to all the good things which have been said of it. Nothing can exceed in romantic beauty the appearance of Interlaken as you enter it from the lake. Whirling through a long street of huge and quaint Swiss cottages, with their steep, projecting roofs, evidently built with a view to the severe winters of this region, we at length emerge into a beautiful avenue, shaded by broad-spreading trees, and lined with hotels, *pensions*, and stores for the sale of Swiss fancy articles. On the left hand flows the river Aar, connecting the lakes Thun and Brienz. Towards the west are the snow-clad summits of the Bernese Alps, and through an opening between two inferior mountains, rises that wondrous beauty, the Jungfrau, to the height of 13,720 feet above the sea; brilliant with its vast glaciers, and crowned with the snows of an endless winter. It is impossible to tire of that scene. Day after day we look upon it with freshening interest, and even now, among the pleasant memories of the Old World, that lovely valley smiles before me with all its quiet beauty, as distinct and clear as when my eye first gazed upon it.

We wonder not that Interlaken has become the favorite resort of Europe. In fact, it is an English settlement, with English customs, manners, and habits. One of the most practicable and delightful excursions which can be made, is that to the valley of Lauterbrunnen. It was one of the sights of Switzerland which I had most wished to see. The ride thither is full of romantic interest, growing more and more wildly beautiful, until we turn into a valley bounded by huge cliffs, which approach each other as we pass onward, until they seem almost to meet. The view at this point is indescribably grand. The road winds along the banks of a roaring mountain torrent, fed by the glaciers and snows of the Alps. As the valley gradually opens before us, its beautiful cascades, falling like silver threads from the mountain peaks, form one of its most attractive features. Shepherd boys, with their rude Alpine horns, are awaking the echoes of these huge cliffs, which take up the wild strains and repeat them from height to height, until they die away in music so sweet and soft that it seems as if an angel's harp were catching the notes upon its strings, and bearing them heavenward.

Passing a collection of Swiss cottages, with a hotel and a neat village church, we approach the wonderful fall of the Staubbach, which comes pouring down from the height of nine hundred feet. Long ere it reaches the valley below it is broken into silver threads, and falls so gently that its murmur seems like the rustling of a bridal veil, which nature has thrown over the scene. Byron, in his Drama of Manfred, has described it, investing it with the peculiar hues with which his strange mind looked upon nature:

> "It is not noon—the sun-bow's rays still arch
> The torrent with the many hues of heaven:
> And roll the sheeted silver's waving column
> O'er the crags, head-long, perpendicular;
> And flings its lines of foaming light along,
> And to and fro, like the pale courser's tail—
> The giant steed to be bestrode by Death,
> As told in the Apocalypse!"

Besides this fall, there are thirty more, which come falling from the clouds to mingle with the torrent which is hurrying downward toward the rivers and lakes below. But we cannot linger here, except to obtain a few souvenirs of the place, and to fill our minds and memories with the wondrous wildness and beauty of the scene. We spent a pleasant Sabbath at Interlaken, and listened to a sound, evangelical discourse, from the English chaplain. It was most touchingly beautiful and affecting, to hear offered up, in that far-distant land, prayers for the Queen of England, " and thy servant, the President of the United States;" the words fell most gratefully on our ears. It was hard to leave this lovely valley. But a mountain storm, which, we were told, might last many days, was gathering upon us. The clouds began to shut down upon the Jungfrau and hide her beauties from us; and so, turning away, we were, in a few hours, at Bern,—after another sail upon the lake of Thun, a view of the picturesque town which bears its name, and a ride of two or three hours in the cars.

Bern is a quaint old Swiss town, with two or three long streets, built with solid and heavy colonnades, which we found very comfortable to shop or walk under during a storm. The city stands upon a hill overlooking the Aar, and has several fine public buildings and monuments. It contains about 27,000 inhabitants. The traditions in regard to its early history are, that it was founded in 1191 by the Duke Berchthold, who killed a monstrous bear upon the spot, and who began there a city which he called Bern (the Bear) in honor of that event. The Bear seems certainly to be the patron saint of Bern

—if an animal can properly be called a patron saint, and bears raised to that dignity—for almost every monument or fountain has a statue of one. The city is abundantly supplied with water, and with fountains of most queer device. Among these is the Ogre Fountain, representing a monster devouring a child, while his pockets are filled, like a cannibal Santa Claus, with a number of others, of whom he evidently intends making a meal. There are, also, several curious clocks, one of which has a number of figures moving by machinery, so that, when the clock strikes, a procession of men and animals moves out; a cock flaps his wings, and crows; Time turns his hour-glass; another puppet strikes the hours upon a bell, and the king stretches, gapes, and lowers his sceptre. There is a fine promenade, built upon a platform, one hundred and eight feet above the Aar, from which may be had a magnificent view of the Bernese Alps, which, when seen at sunset, reflect the light from their snowy peaks, and present a scene of rare beauty even in Switzerland.

Taking the cars from Bern, a few hours' ride

brings us to Lucerne, and the lake of the Four Cantons, memorable for the stirring scenes enacted there, giving Liberty and Independence to Switzerland. The city itself, though small, has many objects of interest,—such as its antique bridges, with their quaint paintings, numbered by hundreds, filling the triangular spaces under the roofs. Here, also, is the Lion monument, carved from the solid rock where it stands. This statue was intended to commemorate the names of the Swiss Guard of Louis XVI., who fell during one of the revolutions in France. The Lion lies in a grotto forty-four feet long, and is itself twenty-eight feet in length. But the great beauty of Lucerne is the lake, and the scenery which surrounds it. Taking the steamer, and sailing up toward Fluellin, we pass through a succession of scenes of the most interesting character. Upon the right rises Mt. Pilatus, the violent storms which gather around it being thought the perturbations of Pilate, who, tradition says, wandered hither and drowned himself in the lake. Though how on earth he reached here, I have never learned. On the left stands the Rigi, from whose summit may be had, in clear weather, the most extensive panorama of Switzerland. We would gladly have endured the toil of the ascent, had the clouds given any sign of settled weather. But we remembered the sad experience of those who had before made the attempt, and whose sorrow found utterance in the following poetical effusion, written, it is said, in the Album at the summit:

> "Nine weary, up-hill miles we sped,
>   The setting sun to see;
>   Sulky and grim he went to bed;
>   Sulky and grim went we!
>   Seven sleepless hours we tossed—and then,
>   The rising sun to see,
>   Sulky and grim we rose again,
>   Sulky and grim rose he."

We had no special desire to subject our temper and patience to this tax, and so we passed on, with new beauties ever opening before us, toward the head of the lake. Bold and rocky promontories stand in clear outline upon its borders, and send their giant shadows over its waters. At the foot of the Rigi is a slip of land, upon the steep slope of the hill, about two miles wide by three long, which for a long time formed an independent state. A very small state that, yet it is a fact that for four centuries its inhabitants preserved their independence. Passing on from this point, we enter upon a wild and magnificent scene, where the lake is hemmed in by vast mountains, whose tops shine with perpetual snows, and whose awful and rugged sides seem only fitted for the home of storms and the eyrie of the eagle. This is the scene where Tell bravely fought for liberty, and freed his country from the yoke of the oppressor. Upon a point of rock stands a chapel, marking the spot upon which he sprang from the boat in which Gesler was bearing him to prison. The story of this escape and the death of Gesler, is familiar to every school-boy. After those memorable scenes,—of the tearing down of the tyrant's cap, the shooting the apple from the boy's head, and the discovery of that other arrow which was intended for the tyrant's heart,—Tell was made a captive, and taken by Gesler across the lake to the castle in which he was to be confined. During their passage a most violent storm came up, and Gesler, in alarm, asked Tell to manage the boat. The Swiss hero guided the little craft so well that its stern touched the shore first, and he sprang out and made good his escape, after lodging an arrow in the heart of the tyrant. This chapel was erected in 1388, not long after Tell's death, and it is the scene of an annual gathering and festival to commemorate the event. The scenery around is sublime. The mountains rising above it, present a panorama awfully grand and majestic.

Returning to Lucerne, a car-ride of a few hours brings us to Basle and the Rhine, upon whose swift and arrowy waters it stands. It has the quaint appearance of an old German town, with its steep-roofed houses and churches. Here it was that the famous council was held in the fifteenth century, and in the ancient minster are preserved many relics of Erasmus, whose labors were here given to the cause of the Protestant Church. The cathedral towers are odd, and a most queer-looking bell hangs on the outside of one of them. Quaint figures and carvings decorate it, within and without, and its whole appearance is in keeping with its great age. Crossing the river, we take the cars for Baden-Baden, one of the most celebrated watering places of Germany.

The country is level and comparatively uninteresting, except as it abounds in countless vineyards and farms, and skirts the borders of the Black Forest, so long famous in German legends. Passing Fribourg, whose tall minster-spire is a prominent feature of the town, and catching a distant view of the cathedral of Strasbourg, in a few hours we arrive at Baden-Baden, a city of about 6,000 inhabitants, and which lies chiefly upon the slope of a hill, from whose summit may be obtained a view of almost unsurpassed beauty and extent.

Here stand the ruins of an ancient castle, at which, until the year 1741, the Dukes of Baden resided. A new one has since been built, lower down the hill, where the present Duke dwells, and which is open to visitors. It is a tasteful chateau, but beneath it are dungeons, gloomy and fearful, filled with the sad emblems of ancient tyranny and oppression. Winding our way downward, under the direction of the castellan, we come to chambers which were once filled with instruments of torture, a few of which still remain. The doors are of solid stone, and of great thickness, and their closing sound must have fallen dreadfully upon the ear of the prisoner whose fate hung upon the will of a brutal tyrant. Every spot reminded us of those days of darkness when the strong ruled the weak, and violence and oppression stood in the place of liberty and law. We passed through these doors into a vaulted space, and entered the chamber where the prisoners were tried and condemned. And we shuddered as we thought of the scenes which had here been enacted.

Near the castle are 13 hot springs bursting from the ground, which so heat the earth that the place is called Hell—a name, as we shall see, better applied to a much more attractive resort. The water is conveyed by pipes to the Trinke Halle, where it is drawn off for use. Large rows of shops for the sale of various articles line the avenue to the famous *Converzations haus*, which is one of the great features of Baden.

Everything sold in Vanity Fair may be found in these shops. The saloon is nothing more than an immense gambling-house, fitted up in the most magnificent manner, in which, besides numerous private parlors and rooms, there are two large halls for gambling, and these are the resort of many of the nobility of Europe. Here they sit, hour after hour, staking their money— their characters gone long ago. In front of the house is a large square, where a splendid band of music gives evening concerts. In the porch, as you enter, hang the hats and opera-cloaks of ladies who have come to spend their evening and their money. Passing through a splendid hall, where a roulette table is surrounded by men and women, you enter a second hall, where a crowd of both sexes are seated, eagerly engaged in the game of *Rouge et Noir*. Piles of money are lying before them; one man deals the cards, and calls out red or black, as one or the other happens to turn up; and the four *croupiers*, with small rakes, push out or bring in the money which has been won or lost. Strict silence is observed, and hour after hour that group are busy at their terrible amusement. Never did I see such expressions of countenance as at that table, as the players placed large rolls of gold coin upon it, and at a turn of the cards, either lost or won. I confess that I never could see what particular amusement there is in card-playing. It seems like a stupid and idle way of spending time, and to my mind argues a want of good sense. But gambling predicates an utter absence of every noble and manly virtue and principle. It is said that this place is let to a company (who also farm out similar rights at other watering-places) for $15,000 annually, and that, besides this, the company agree to expend a much larger sum in improvements about the city. It is a sad sight to watch these groups of men and women, whether they gain or lose, and to think that, in a spot of so much beauty, there should be such appliances for crime.

Leaving Baden-Baden, we proceed by rail to Heidelburg, whose chief attraction is the magnificent ruin crowning the hill, and affording one of the most splendid specimens in Europe of a castle of the feudal ages. Taking a carriage we ascend an almost precipitous hill, lined with quaint old German houses, and crowded with women and children, many of whom would have been none the worse off for a little soap and water. Our driver could speak French, but every one around us was uttering German, which, when spoken as musically as possible, resembles more the sound made by the filing of a cross-cut saw than anything I can imagine. At the castle, a bright and intelligent young woman became our cicerone, led us over the ruins, and disposed of some very fine views of the spot. This vast and noble building, after having been three times burned, and having sustained ten sieges, was again set on fire by lightning, just after it had been fitted up as a residence for its royal proprietors: since which time (1764) it has remained a ruin.

Pausing on our way down, to look at the venerable church of St. Peter's, to whose door Jerome, of Prague, long before Luther, nailed his Theses, declaring his dissent from the faith of Rome, we resume our place in the cars, and, passing through Worms, in sight of the cathedral where Luther nobly affirmed the doctrines of the Reformation, we stop, for the night, at Mayence, whence the boats down the Rhine take their departure. The current at this place runs at about five or six knots or miles an hour. We pass a boat whose paddles are ceaselessly beating the water, and yet it never advances. It is anchored here, and is employed in grinding corn. At Mayence we meet with many objects worthy of our attention. It was here that Guttenburg was born, to whose genius we are indebted for the invention of movable type, and his monument in bronze stands in an open square in the city. His first printing-office is also to be seen. There is a noble cathedral here, built in the tenth and eleventh centuries, and filled with monuments and statues. Across the river is stretched the first bridge of boats with which we meet, and which affords a very comfortable and safe transit. It is in the form of a bow, in order to better resist the force of the current, and is so arranged with machinery, as to allow the passage down and up the river of other boats. Here lie at anchor a large number of tide mills, like that we have just described, seeming like some old-fashioned steamboats attempting to ascend the river.

Early in the morning, we take passage in one of the numerous Rhine boats, for Cologne. A large number of these vessels leave, every day, both morning and evening. As regards comforts and conveniences, they might be greatly improved, for they scarcely excel one of our ordinary tug-boats in accommodations. They have no cabins, except down below. You must eat on deck, even in the rain; and, as if to inconvenience you in every possible way, they put their small boats just where they will intercept your view. If you ask them why they don't have American steamers, they reply that "American boats blow up!" The Dutchmen prefer safety to comfort, and we don't know but they have made the best if not the most pleasant choice. There is a fine chance, however, for an enterprising Yankee to make a fortune, if he will take American models out upon the Rhine. Four boats would be enough, two for day and two for night travel. We might teach the Germans something, and might learn from them, too, for that matter. We should be willing to exchange ideas, and both parties would be benefited.

Much of the interest of a sail down the Rhine depends upon the associations connected with it. For, in the first place, the Rhine takes its rise from the glaciers and snows of the Alps, which also feed its countless tributary streams. Then, it is nine hundred miles long, six hundred of which are navigable. With the exception of that part which lies between Bingen and Drachenfels, the scenery is tame and comparatively uninteresting. Between these two points there is a marked resemblance to the Highlands of our own Hudson river. Contrasting the whole of the Rhine with the Hudson, or the valley of the Connecticut—which I think the most beautiful in the world—or the majestic St. Lawrence—which every one ought to see—I cannot but believe that much of the admiration which has been lavished upon it is due to the contrasts it presents between its tame and flat shores, and the splendid gorge above Drachenfels, and partly from the romance which is thrown over it by the venerable castles and ruins which meet the eye at every turn, and with each of which some German legend is connected. The numerous vineyards which line its sides and grace every hill which rises above it, also add much to its beauty; while many picturesque towns and villages, or noble fortresses, rising upon commanding elevations, contribute to its interest. The Germans certainly do understand agriculture, and they are a most wonderful people in this respect. The vineyards from which are produced the many celebrated wines known in the vocabulary of the epicure, are grown upon terraces, overhanging the river, and present a very pretty appearance when seen from it. When they cannot find soil enough among the rocks, they hang out baskets of earth, and cultivate the vine in them.

As we pass downward by the celebrated Bingen on the Rhine, a small square tower is seen rising from an island, just below and near the junction of the Nahe with the Rhine. It is the famous Mouse Tower of Bishop Hatto, of whom tradition tells this story: During a seven years' famine, the Bishop, in whose barn was an abundance of grain, invited the starving and clamorous poor to enter his granaries and help themselves. Upon a set day they came, and when they had filled one of his barns, he set it on fire, and consumed the poor wretches, presuming that the country would be very much obliged to him for burning the rats who only ate up the corn. The next day news came that the real rats were eating up his grain, and, soon after, that, having devoured all they had found, they were about proceeding to eat up his Lordship also. To avoid such a fate he fled in haste to this tower, and laid himself down to sleep in peace. But his cat soon awakened him with the intelligence that the rats were swimming the Rhine. He fell upon his knees in terror, as he heard them gnawing away at the door, and saw them pouring in at the windows; and after whetting their teeth against the stones, they proceeded to finish the amiable bishop himself, as a proper punishment for his enormous crimes!

As we pass onward, we plunge into the deep gorge of the Rhine, made by the passage of a range of mountains across the river. Here begin the series of castles built by the robbers and highwaymen of the feudal ages, whose posterity are now the princes and nobility of Germany. Here they entrenched themselves, and lived in security upon the plunder which they gained from travellers, and to which they affixed the name of "toll," to give it respectability, but which was nothing better than black-mail or robbery.

Following the rapid current of the Rhine, we pass the bleak and bare precipice of Leirleiburg, with a remarkable echo, used by the German students for a bit of humor, to obtain an answer to the question, who is Burgomaster of Oberweisel? You must know that "Esel" in German means an "ass," or a "stupid fellow." So the students ask, "Who is the Burgomaster of Oberweisel?" "Esel," replies the echo, and the students are answered. Not far above us seven rocks jut out above the waters, into which it is said that seven beautiful coquettes, who had turned the heads and broken the hearts of all the beaux on the Rhine, were thrown for their obstinacy. Still farther down stands the summer palace of the King of Prussia. Sailing downward, we come to Coblentz, at the junction of the Blue Moselle. Here, upon a commanding elevation, stands the splendid fortress of Ehrenbreitstein, overlooking the city, with which the village below the castle is connected by a bridge of boats. This vast citadel is the Gibralter of the Rhine. It fell into the hands of the French after a protracted siege, and was blown up by them when they left it after the peace. It is to this that Byron alludes in these words:

> "Here Ehrenbreitstein with her shattered wall
> Black with the miner's blast, upon her height
> Yet shows of what she was, when shell and ball
> Rebounding idly on her strength did light:
> A tower of victory! from whence the flight
> Of baffled foes was watched along the plain:
> But peace destroyed what war could never blight,
> And laid those proud roofs bare to summer's rain,
> On which the iron shower for years had pour'd in vain!"

But this fortress is now kept in perfect repair

by the Prussians, is capable of holding 100,000 men, and its magazines can contain provisions for a siege of ten years, with 8,000 soldiers. Four hundred cannons defend the walls, which are of great strength, and seem, in their present state, to defy the assaults of war.

At this point the gorge of the river terminates, but the Rhine retains much of its romantic beauty and picturesque castles and ruins, until we reach the Seven Mountains, the most beautiful and remarkable of which is the famed Drachenfels, from whose summit the valley of the Rhine may be seen as far down as Cologne, and where one feels, as he gazes upon that scene of beauty, the power of the poet's song:

> "The castle craig of Drachenfels
> Frowns o'er the wide and winding Rhine,
> Whose breast of water broadly swells
> Between the banks which bear the vine,
> And hills all rich with blossomed trees.
> And fields, which promise corn and wine,
> And scattered cities, crowning these,
> Whose far white walls along them shine,
> Have strewed a scene, which I should see
> With double joy, wert thou with me!"

From this point to the city of Cologne the scenery is tame and uninteresting. At Cologne we find a city which is just beginning to recover from a long and fearful paralysis of trade, but whose history is full of interest, and whose churches and monuments well repay a visit. A bridge of boats crosses the Rhine here, and the railroad company have just completed a viaduct of great strength and beauty. This city was a Roman camp when Tacitus wrote his annals, and, as lately as the French Revolution, the higher classes called themselves "patricians," and the town-banners bore the Roman inscription of S. P. Q. R. Owing to the bigotry and intolerance of its Popish rulers, trade gradually left Cologne and found other marts. Meanwhile its churches and religious institutions increased, until it was filled with ecclesiastics and beggars. The restrictions under which it languished have now been removed, and the city is gradually awakening from its long and death-like stupor. It contains numerous churches, which, in their decorations and relics, seem to reproduce the scenes of Italy.

First in interest is the cathedral, or *Dom Kirche*, which might properly be called the church of magnificent intentions. It was begun in the year 1248, and is still incomplete. When finished it will be one of the finest gothic structures in the world. The choir is completed, and is a gem of beauty. Its ceiling is 161 feet high, and its stained-glass windows, its stupendous columns and buttresses, and its beautiful frescoes and ornaments, combine to make it scarcely surpassed in Europe, and show us what will be the magnificence of the church when finished. In a small chapel, behind the choir, are three skulls, profusely decorated and surrounded by articles of great value. These skulls are said to be those of the Magi, who brought their gifts to the infant Saviour. The church of St. Peter's is decorated with an altarpiece by Rubens, representing the Crucifixion of the Apostle. In the church of St. Ursula, the walls and columns are covered with the bones of 11,000 virgins, who, it is said, were slaughtered at Cologne by the Huns, because they refused to violate their vows of celibacy There the bones are, grinning at you from every side,—a spectacle more ghastly than sublime.

The manufacture of Cologne-water, which has made this city famous, seems to be an absolute necessity to counteract the horribly impure atmosphere, which every one breathes in the filthy streets. Coleridge declares that he encountered sixty or seventy distinct smells, besides several decided odors of still worse character and name. As the result of his experience, he wrote:

> "Ye nymphs who reign o'er sewers and sinks,
> The river Rhine, it is well known,
> Doth wash your city of Cologne;
> But, tell me, nymphs, what power divine,
> Shall henceforth wash the river Rhine!"

Jean Maria Farina is the great manufacturer of Cologne-water, but as there is a score of that name in the city, it is rather difficult to know which is the "genuine original."

Resuming our route down the river, which, from this point, is wholly flat and uninteresting, a night's sail, in a most uncomfortable boat utterly unfitted for sleeping, brings us to Arnheim, the first town in Holland, whence we take the cars for Amsterdam.

Everything in this wonderful country seems

to be the reverse of all which we have hitherto seen. A greater part of it has been rescued from the sea, at an immense outlay of time, labor, and money, and is preserved from inundation only by constant vigilance and effort. Large dykes, filled in with reeds and mud, keep out the water. Canals make a perfect network throughout the country, and seem to be essential to the perfection of every city, hamlet, and farm. As we approach Amsterdam, its numerous windmills, their sails flying around in the stiff breeze, form a prominent feature of the landscape. The city is traversed by four great canals, which are intersected by various smaller ones, by which it is divided into ninety-five islands, connected by three hundred bridges. The town is built upon piles driven down deep through layers of sand and bog, into the firm soil beneath. Along the canal are fine rows of trees, and the houses have the usual quaint appearance of an old Dutch town, with gable-ends to the street, and roofs which run up, like steeples, to a great height, and are surmounted with the old conventional vane. The city contains a population of 212,000, and is, in most parts, a very model of neatness. One of the queer "institutions" of Amsterdam is a coach or cart on runners, by the side of which walks the driver, with a rag which he occasionally dips in oil, and applies under the runners, to lessen the friction and make its motion more easy. Heavy burdens, however, are conveyed by the canals. Just opposite the city begins the ship canal, fifty miles in length, which forms the great highway between Amsterdam and the ocean.

The palace is a vast building on piles, with many rooms well furnished and richly decorated. The grand hall is lined with pure Italian marble, and is one hundred and twenty feet in length by one hundred in height. The churches of Amsterdam, though stripped of their former ornaments, present some noble specimens of architecture. The ministers wear a singular and quaint black gown, in the fashion of the Puritans in the time of Charles I. It is a sort of cloak, decorated with a ruff around the neck. The people sit with their hats on during service, like the members of the British House of Parliament. The minster contains a noble organ, of great power and rich tone. Along the harbor one observes many pavilions, to which the citizens come in their boats, and where they sit and smoke their pipes, and drink their beer and coffee, during the summer evenings.

From Amsterdam to Rotterdam, the road passes through a fine farming district, and the eye is charmed with the appearances of thrift and home comfort which everywhere abound. Rotterdam is but a repetition of every other Dutch city, with its canals, its dykes, its windmills, its tiled roofs, its fresh and cleanly-looking women, its unmistakably Dutch physiognomies, its quaint-looking boats, its droll houses, and droller people, that, according to Butler, in his Hudibras:

"——always ply the pump, and never think
They can be safe but at the rate they sink;
That live as if they had been run aground,
And, when they die, are cast away and drowned.
A land that rides at anchor, and is moored!
In which they do not live, but—go aboard!"

With all that is quaint and strange, Holland

is a country which deserves the respect of the world. It is a wonderful example of the triumph of industry and science over nature. Its merchants have forced commerce and trade thither. Its farmers are growing rich upon land which they have reclaimed from the sea. Its ships float above the house-tops. Its croaking frogs in the marshes look down upon the swallows which twitter in the chimneys! Holland was the early home of the Reformation. It has encouraged learning and freedom, and long before our Revolution it had a liberal and just government, modelled, like that of the church, upon a scheme which divided the power between the rulers and the people. Nor can one fail of seeing everywhere around him, as he journeys through the country, that industry, order, intelligence and virtue, which are the essential elements of a nation's greatness.

Leaving Rotterdam by steamer, we proceed by a pleasant sail to Antwerp. A number of cities are passed on our way, among which is the famous Dort, or Dordricht, celebrated as the place of meeting of the Synod which settled the doctrine of the Reformed Church of Holland. We pause at Antwerp, a fine and prosperous commercial city, to visit the cathedral, in which hangs the celebrated altar-piece, by Rubens, of the Descent from the Cross. The pulpits and confessionals of this church are of rare beauty. The cathedral itself is of great size and fine proportions.

Leaving Antwerp just at sundown, a pleasant ride of two hours brings us to Brussels, which, in its neatness, taste and fashion, is a miniature Paris. Our first business in the morning is to visit the battle-ground of Waterloo. We pursue the same route which the English army took. A few miles out we were joined by Sergeant Mundy—a brother-in-law of the former cicerone—whose graphic description of the action adds greatly to the interest of a visit to that spot. A vast mound, two hundred feet high, has been thrown up as a monument of the dreadful conflict. We inspected the whole field: the spot where the battle began; the farm-house so often retaken; the trench before it in which the wounded hid from the cannon balls; the spot where the Old Guard stood and melted away before the stern armies of England. Everything was marked out for us by our guide, and we rehearsed the entire battle. We returned from this spot, filled with these mighty memories, and recalling this most tremendous conflict of modern times, and the brave men, gathered in Belgium's capital, who marched forth over this very road—to death.

> "And Ardennes waves above them her green leaves,
> Dewy with Nature's tear-drops, as they pass,
> Grieving, if aught inanimate e'er grieves,
> Over the unreturning brave,—alas!
> E'er evening to be trodden like the grass,
> Which now beneath them, but above shall grow
> In its next verdure, when this fiery mass
> Of living valor, rolling on the foe,
> And burning with high hope, shall moulder, cold and low.

We spent a day in looking over Brussels, and then taking the cars for Ostend passed through a country which was giving every indication of thrift and industry.

XII.

ENGLAND.

A SMALL and utterly comfortless steamer received us at Ostend, a city exceedingly well contrived to make us happy to leave the Continent. For the last time my passport was inspected by the authorities of Belgium, after which, as a sort of refreshing revenge, I thrust it down into the darkest corner of my carpet bag. As we steamed away from the harbor, a most uncomfortable swell began to give to us indications of what we were to expect, and as the wind and waves seemed determined to make a night of it, most of the passengers found it necessary to retire to the cabin, and the sailors were glad to get as far as possible from the forward deck, which for several hours was completely washed by the heavy seas which came tumbling in upon us without so much as saying "By your leave." It was slightly amusing to see a lady, who had been boasting somewhat of her nautical experiences, and her freedom from the usual penalties which the sea exacted, stretched out upon a lounge in all the horror of sea-sickness, with an awful visage which betokened anything but a sound and healthy state of the stomach.

At last we reach England, pass the lighthouse of Dover, the ship hauls into her berth, the officers of the customs take charge of our baggage, and we find our way up a huge flight of stairs to the street, and to a hotel near by. There is an air of comfort about an English inn, which one finds nowhere on the Continent,—at least we did not. There is a tempting look about those huge and juicy rounds of beef which the waiter sets down before a hungry traveller that is utterly indescribable. And the rosy-cheeked, fresh-looking and good-natured maid-servant, with her pretty white cap and apron, who attends to your comforts, and bustles about all in smiles and ribbons, looks so thoroughly

English, that a traveller from the Continent would know he was in England if he had been taken there while asleep.

Dover is a city of about twenty-two thousand souls, encompassed by a splendid range of hills and cliffs of chalk, upon which are several important fortresses. The castle is an immense structure, which is supposed to have been founded by the Romans, and which was afterwards added to and improved by the Normans and Saxons. Overlooking the sea is an immense cliff of chalk, three hundred and fifty feet high. It is on this spot that Shakspeare has laid some of the scenes in his stupendous tragedy of King Lear. It was this cliff that Edgar described to his blind father;

> . . . . . "How fearful
> And dizzy 'tis to cast one's eyes so low.
> . . . The murmuring surge
> That on the unnumbered idle pebbles chafe
> Cannot be heard so high. I'll look no more
> Lest my brain turn, and the deficient sight
> Topple down headlong."

Passing through the tunnel under this cliff we travel through a country of exceeding beauty, where every inch of land seems to be in the highest state of cultivation. As the road enters London it passes over a series of arches built above the housetops in many places, and landing us within a moment's walk of the famous London Bridge.

The Sabbath following our arrival we attended services in Westminster Abbey, the place of all others we had most desired to see in London, for its monumental collections, and as the repository of the dust of England's mighty dead. A small part only of the Abbey is appropriated to religious services.

We took an early opportunity in the succeeding week to spend a part of a day in visiting this vast edifice. Its origin dates back to the seventh century, from which time it has been enlarged and beautified until it has reached its present stately appearance. It is built in the form of a Latin cross, three hundred and seventy-five feet by two hundred, with a height of one hundred and one feet. The interior of the church presents a fine example of Gothic architecture, but it is the wondrous collection of monuments which forms the glory of this pile.

Beginning at the Poet's corner, we pass thro' a vast array of noble memorials which show that England does not forget to honor the memory of departed worth and genius. Almost every form of monumental sculpture is here seen. Addison is surrounded by the Muses. Handel rests with his left arm upon a group of musical instruments, listening with fixed attention to a seraph's harp, while before him is a scroll on which is engraved the theme of one of his noblest songs, "I know that my Redeemer liveth." Shakspeare stands leaning upon a pedestal on which appears the grand and sublime utterance of his Prospero in the Tempest:

> "The cloud-capt towers, the gorgeous palaces,
> The solemn temples, the great globe itself,
> Yea, all which it inherit, shall dissolve,
> And, like this unsubstantial pageant, faded,
> Leave not a rack behind."

A sculptured tablet with the quaint epitaph, "O rare Ben Johnson," is the memorial of that famed poet. Passing into the north transept, magnificent monuments and statues to the memory of Pit, Fox, Canning, and Sir Isaac Newton, and a host of the great names of England

and the world surround you everywhere. But the most interesting portion of the edifice is found in the chapels which commence with the Poet's corner, and fill up the space in the south transept of the cathedral. In the chapel of St. Edward, are twenty monuments of the nobility of England, next to which is the chapel of St. Nicholas, with a large altar tomb in the centre, to the memory of the parents of the Duke of Buckingham. But the great wonder of this structure is the chapel of Henry VII. It was begun in 1512 by that monarch, who was buried in the place not long after its completion. A flight of steps leads to it; it consists of a central aisle, with five smaller chapels at the end. The principal object is the lofty tomb of Henry VII and his queen, Elizabeth. It is admirably executed, and ornamented with the statues of saints. Upon a slab of black marble lie the effigies of the royal pair. As we pass around the chapel, we notice the noble monuments of Queen Elizabeth; of the two princes murdered by Richard; of Mary Queen of Scots; of Margaret Douglass, the mother of Lord Darnley.

Here, too, are laid the remains of George II and Caroline, whose ashes lie mingled in one common grave. The stalls of the chapel are of richly carved oak. Passing away from this mausoleum of the mighty dead, we visit the chapel of St. Paul, with its altar tomb of Ludowick Robsart, the standard-bearer of Edward V at the battle of Agincourt, and beautiful statues of Bramley, the privy counsellor of the queen at the trial of Mary Queen of Scots, and of Watt, whose genius has made his name immortal.

The chapel of Edward the Confessor is rich in historic recollections. His mausoleum, is in the centre of the chapel, and surrounding it are the tombs of Edward I and III, Henry III and V, Philip, and Eleanor, the noble consort of Edward I.

Just opposite the Abbey is the vast pile of buildings devoted to the use of the British Parliament, and where we had the pleasure of listening to an interesting debate in the House of Lords upon the India Question.

The arrangement of the House differs greatly from that of our noble Capitol at Washington.

The seats are on either side of the presiding officer, who occupies the woolsack, behind which is the throne appropriated to her majesty in her visits to the House of Lords. The new Houses of Parliament stand upon the Thames, and have a river front of nine hundred feet. They are magnificent buildings, well worthy the nation whose government here has its centre. There are three principal towers, the largest and most imposing of which is the Victoria tower, through which her majesty enters the building, and which communicates with the Norman porch, so called from the frescoe illustrations of the history of the Norman kings. If we pass eastward from this point down the Strand, and the streets that are its continuation, and turn down a narrow court to the right, we come to the famous Temple, the home of the legal profession for generations. Here are quiet nooks where for ages the great men of England lived and thought. Here Chaucer wrote, Raleigh studied, Goldsmith lived and died, and Cooke, Seldon, Beaumont, Burke, Johnson, and Cooper achieved an immortality of fame. Here stands the Temple church, occupied by the benchers and students of law, and rich with its quaint monuments of the old knights who founded the church in the year 1185. The choral services here are said to be unsurpassed in London. Emerging from this spot, we pause at Temple Bar, the only relic of the old London Wall in this direction. This is the western boundary of the city built by Sir Christopher Wren, and having in niches, statues of Elizabeth and James I, and Charles I and II. Here the heads of executed traitors used to be hung until as late as 1773.

On certain occasions a sort of child's play is acted here by Royalty and the Lord Mayor of London. The Queen, on driving toward the city, finds the gates closed against her, the herald then sounds a trumpet, when the Lord Mayor and Corporation demand her pleasure— on being informed that the Queen wishes to enter the city, these very worthy gentlemen proceed to give her the keys, the gates fly open, and the procession moves on. The chief difference between this ceremony and that sometimes enacted by the aldermen of our own metropolis, of presenting a stranger with the freedom of the city, is that, in London it is part of a time-honored custom, and performed with the dignity and respect which becomes a noble queen, and a nobler woman, while with us the whole thing is a farce, too often followed by scenes of riot and drinking, which do not disgrace the actors in it simply because they are already sunk so low, as to make it impossible to sink lower in the regard of the public.

Passing from Temple Bar, we enter upon the haunts of business, where every step we take recalls to us some new idea of the immense wealth of this mighty city. Yonder is the Bank of England, covering an area of eight acres of ground, with its buildings and offices, giving employment to eight hundred clerks, whose annual salaries amount to about $1,100,000. Hard by is the Royal Exchange, in the front of which stands an equestrian statue of the Duke of Wellington, and from which centre the commerce of the world is regulated. Turn where we will at this point, we enter streets whose names are the very synonymes of business. There is Cornhill glittering with jewelry shops, and Leadenhall street, where stand the massive buildings of the East India Company, and in a narrow passage called Capel street, is the Stock Exchange, with its gamblers, its lame ducks, its bulls, and its bears. Passing onward toward the Thames, we come under the shadow of Old St. Paul's, only one hundred feet shorter than St. Peter's of Rome—modelled after that famous structure, and filled with statues of the great men of England. Its interior loses much of its effect by the screen which shuts off one of the naves of the church for the purpose of religious services which are held here daily. Turning out of our way a moment, to visit an ancient church in Bread street, we pause to read an inscription upon its side, which informs us that in that old church Milton was baptized. The graceful eulogy of Dryden is added beneath this notice:

> "Three poets in three distant ages born,
> Greece, Italy, and England did adorn;
> The first in loftiness of thought surpassed;
> The next in majesty; in both the last:
> The force of nature could no farther go,
> To make the third she joined the other two."

As we pass on, we pause to look in upon another ancient and venerable church, whose chimes are ringing now as they were when Whittington heard them—the old chimes of Bow-bells—which still seem to say, "Turn again, Whittington, Lord Mayor of London." Making our way through endless mazes of streets, we come to the monument built to commemorate the great fire which once swept over this part of the city. Passing still onward, we come at length to the Tower, whose history is almost the history of England, so intimately is it connected with the scenes which have marked its grand events. Obtaining tickets at the entrance to the grounds, we are guided by a person dressed in the style of a beef-eater of the olden time. It is useless to attempt a description of the emotions which stir within a man who has English blood in his veins, and who has read the history of that nation, as he enters this spot. Once a fortress, then a palace, then a prison, and now the grand state show-house of England—we are carried back to the dawn of her national greatness. Yonder, by the very gate at which we enter, were found the bodies of the murdered princes sacrificed to the ambition of Richard III. There stand the effigies of warriors, in the armor and dress of every age. Yonder is the chapel before whose altar are buried the wives of Henry VIII, who fell by the axe, victims of his cruel jealousy. Here are the tombs of Essex, who was the favorite of Elizabeth; and Lady Jane Grey and her husband. Here is the dungeon where Sir Walter Raleigh was confined, and just before it is the block on which poor Anne Boleyn, and others, laid their heads, and the marks of the axe are still upon it. In the Beauchamp tower are the autographs of many of the prisoners who were brought here to await their death. Here the Earl of Warwick wrote his name, and the Duke of Clarence, and underneath is the word *Jane*, placed there by the gentle Lady Jane Grey. Yonder the two princes were murdered, and there the Duke of Clarence was drowned in a butt of Malmsey wine. The arrangement of ancient arms cannot fail to interest the visitor. Every conceivable weapon of offence and defence, from the earliest ages to the present time, line the walls, and are so placed as to produce a most pleasing effect. It would seem impossible that such objects could be placed in such beautiful combinations. They are an epitome of warlike engines of every age and nation—the armor of mail, the battle-axe, the spear, the lance, the pike, and the halberd of the middle ages, are here contrasted with the splendid arms of the present time. There is a spell about this wonderful building which seems to shut out the present and bear one backward along the stream of time to the dark and shadowy past. You think of it as a fortress when it stood as the defence of its monarch, not against the assaults of a foreign foe, but the shock of internal convulsions. It was the centre of power when Stephen usurped the throne, and John and Edward II and Richard II. It was the object of strife when Charles I and his Parliament began the contest, which ended with his life, and through all these revolutions it remained impregnable. Then the scene changes, and we think of it as a palace, and try to reproduce the scenes which have here been witnessed. Here were held the magnificent royal festivities of Henry III and Eleanor. From this spot Richard II went forth in white robes to be crowned at Westminster Abbey, and returned again only at length to resign his crown into the hands of his uncle, and to die a violent death. Here, gay and brilliant tournaments were held in the time of Henry VII. From this spot his Queen Elizabeth, of York, passed to her coronation in splendid robes of white and gold, and again was carried forth in a shroud. In these halls, Henry VIII welcomed his six queens with wonderful and brilliant entertainments. Here came Anne Boleyn, escorted by a splendid civic procession, and in three short years, after having been pronounced guilty of a crime of which history acquits her fully, she lifted up her eyes to heaven and said, "O Father! O Father! Thou who art the Truth and the Life! Thou knowest I have not deserved this death." Here she laid her head upon the block, and closed her short but brilliant career. Here the bloody Mary held her court, and here Elizabeth was welcomed to the throne. From a palace to a prison is a strong contrast, yet it is here presented to the mind in all its startling power. Yonder is the traitor's gate, beneath whose dark and gloomy portals, genius and greatness and royalty have passed from all the dreams of ambition, from the gaiety and splendor of the court to the prison, the fetter, the faggot, and the block. Here the terrible tragedies of Richard III's reign were enacted. Jane Shore was immured within these walls, and released only to die in poverty and suffering, and when the first glimmering light of the Reformation dawned on England, this place became the instrument of Popish tyranny and cruelty. Cobham was shut up here before he was burnt at St. Giles', and Cranmer, Ridley, and Latimer were prisoners in this tower before they were burned at Oxford. But we must leave these scenes and memories, after glancing at the splendid regalia in the jewel-room, used by the sovereigns of England at their Coronation and on State occasions. Here is the anointing spoon of the ancient regalia, and the crown of Charles II, with that of Victoria, and the one to be used by her son, when he shall come to the throne. Leaving this spot, where every object is of intense interest, we visit the tunnel under the Thames, useless, almost, except as a mart for the sale of curiosities; and, emerging from this wonderful work, we take one of the small steamers which ply upon the river, and visit Greenwich with its far-famed Observatory, from which the nautical time of the world is calculated.

Taking the cars to the Crystal Palace at Sydenham, the train lands us under a vast saloon, from which a flight of stairs leads directly to the main building. The grounds are laid out with fine taste, and the fountains are magnificent. One half of the Palace is devoted to ancient art and sculpture, and the other half to all the modern forms of architecture, science and skill. The great transept is decorated with gigantic equestrian statues, fountains, flowers and trees; while on either hand are perfect reproductions of the architecture of every age. Here is a house of Pompeii, and there an Egyptian court, further on is one of Greece and Rome, Assyria and the Alhambra. On every side are magnificent decorations, and works of art and taste, which afford themes of study for days and weeks.

Returning to the city to take a fresh start westward, and, passing through St. James's Square, where stands the palace of the queen, we arrive at Regent's Park, where we spend half a day in looking through the numerous collections of animals, which are finely arranged at the Zoological Gardens, and are provided with the climate and scenery of their native lands. Every variety of bird, reptile, and animal is here to be met with. The vulture and eagle have their rocks and trees in which they are wont to build their nests. The trout swims in his own clear stream of running water; the crocodile basks upon the sand by the water's edge; while the huge hippopotamus sports at the bottom of the pool prepared for his home.

The whole of this vast garden is a noble monument of skill, wealth and intelligence. But the British Museum, which claims our attention, surpasses even this in its vast and varied treasures of knowledge. It is a grand repository of every curiosity of nature and of art, of the past and the present. Immense halls are devoted to Egyptian, Assyrian, Grecian and Roman antiquities. The Library is a magnificent collection of typographical curiosities, containing works of rare beauty and value, manuscripts of great antiquity, and specimens of every form of printing.

The Reading Room is a vast circular Hall, second only to the Pantheon, and fitted up with a library of 80,000 volumes, and reading desks for 300 persons. Here men of literature may come and investigate and study, with as much quiet as if in their own homes. We cannot look over this splendid Museum, and not obtain a new evidence of the wealth and grandeur of a nation which can make such arrangements for the intellectual wants of the people.

But it were utterly useless to attempt anything like a full description of London. My last Sabbath evening was spent in hearing one of its celebrated preachers, Dr. Cumming of the Presbyterian Church. I went early, and was shown to a comfortable seat at once, although usually strangers are compelled to wait until the pew-holders are seated. A vast throng were gathered together and listened with fixed attention to a noble discourse from the Pastor. After service I sent my card to the Dr., and was invited into his study, where I spent a pleasant half hour with him in speaking of the prospects of the Presbyterian Church in England, and of the evidence of the success of the efforts of its ministers and people.

Leaving London by the cars, we visit Hampton Court, which was built by Cardinal Wolsey in the height of his glory and power. The Palace covers about eight acres, and has room for the accommodation of several thousands of guests. The pictures alone, as they are arranged in long halls, number more than one thousand, and a pamphlet of nearly one hundred pages is necessary to give even a general outline of the objects of historic interest which everywhere present themselves. The gardens and walks are of great extent and beauty.

Returning from this spot to London, we take

the cars for Windsor, and are set down within a few minutes walk of the Castle, one of the residences of the Queen. Its history dates back to the time of the Saxon Kings. William the Conqueror built a noble structure, and succeeding kings enlarged, strengthened and beautified it, until it rose to its present shape and size. Edward III was born here, and erected, for the order of the Garter, the Chapel of St. George, which was afterwards replaced by the present church. This is a most interesting spot, filled with the tombs and memorials of the mighty dead. Edward IV is buried here; and here lie the ashes of George III and Queen Charlotte, with all the succeeding monarchs and members of the royal family. A portion of the Castle is devoted to a collection of works of historical interest, and to some fine paintings by the ancient masters.

Leaving Windsor Castle, we cross the Thames in sight of the famous Eton College, and arrive at Oxford, the great seat of learning and literature. In the reign of Alfred, Oxford was a place for schools. Here Wickliffe taught and

Latimer, Ridley and Cranmer died for the faith. A cross in one of the streets marks the spot where the stake stood, and a fine monument near at hand commemorates the event. There are twenty colleges, and five halls, many of great antiquity, in this city. The grounds around them are everything an English student could wish. Our guide, whose breath told of a very strong preference for English beer, with a slight disposition to brandy and whiskey, took us through every part of the College that was worth seeing, even to the dining-room and kitchen. We looked over the Parks with their fine herds of deer, belonging to the " fellows," and they are the only DEARS they are allowed to have while they retain their fellowship, for they must remain bachelors. Here Addison walked and studied, and here many a noble British scholar has lived and thought and prepared for himself an undying fame.

Leaving Oxford, we pass to Stratford on Avon, the home of Shakspeare. As I entered the omnibus I directed the conductor to set us down at the *oldest* inn in the town. I felt that in such a place nothing *new* should be seen on the errand on which I was coming. We were dropped at the Red Horse Inn, the very spot of all others I could have wished to make my home. Nothing could be more comfortable than that cosy chamber into which I was shown, and where I lay down to sleep, and when I arose early the next morning, and entered the snug parlor, the first book on which I laid my hand was the Sketch Book of Washington Irving, and as I opened to his description of Stratford on Avon, I found that I was in the same inn and the same parlor in which he wrote it. Our first visit was to the birth-place of Shakspeare, which, as in the days of Irving, was shown by a garrulous female who usually succeeds in disposing of a number of relics of Stratford, in addition to the entrance fee which she receives. The old chair of Shakspeare is still shown, which, although it has passed through many changes of seats and sides, is still looked on as a sacred relic of the immortal poet. But there is no doubt as to the house where the Bard of Avon first saw the light. Turning away towards the old church, we pass the Guild Hall, in a niche of whose walls is a statue of the Poet, leaning upon his hand, and pointing to a scroll, on which are the beautiful words of his Midsummer Night's Dream—

> "The Poet's eye, in a fine frenzy rolling,
> Doth glance from Heav'n to Earth, from Earth to Heav'n,
> And as imagination bodies forth
> The form of things unknown, the Poet's pen
> Turns them to shapes, and gives to airy nothing
> A local habitation and a name."

Upon the border of the base of the statue are the words—

> "Take him for all in all,
> We ne'er shall look upon his like again."

Passing by the school house where he was educated, we turn down towards the gently sloping banks of the Avon, where stands the old church in which the boy Shakspeare worshipped, and where the immortal Poet is buried. Long avenues of dark trees lead from the main road to the sacred edifice around whose venerable tower the rooks and swallows are flying in countless numbers. Here, amid many monuments, is the tomb of Shakspeare. Upon the wall his bust is placed, and beneath a simple slab his remains are laid. Upon the slab are the well known words:

> Good friend, for Jesus' sake forbeare
> To digg the dust enclosed heare;
> Blest be ye man yt spares these stones,
> And curst be he yt moves my bones."

Turning from the scene, a short ride brings us to the cottage of Ann Hathaway, where Shakspeare found his wife. It is a plain and rude dwelling, but there is a charm thrown around the spot. We enter it, and find the old settle on which he used to rest, and sit down in the broad chimney, where he doubtless often sat and whiled away his evening with the young object of his love. A descendant of the Hathaway family still lives there, although the place has passed out of their hands. Taking the mail stage toward Warwick, we pass the grounds of the Lacy family, before one of whose ancestors the young Shakspeare is said to have been brought for deer-stalking, and whom he has immortalized as his Justice Shallow, in the "Merry Wives of Windsor." As we rode by the spot, a crowd of deer were roaming over the woodlands, bringing forcibly to our mind the scenes in the life of the Poet which drove him forth to London, where his career as a dramatist began. Passing through scenery, which is the very perfection of an English landscape, we reach Warwick with its noble castle, and Kenilworth with its magnificent ruins, the scene of one of Sir Walter Scott's works and possessing a deep interest in its associations with the age of Elizabeth. We paused here for a few hours, to visit this spot and refresh our minds with its memories ; thence by rail to Coventry, through which poor Jack Falstaff was ashamed to march his ragged army; to York, an ancient and venerable town, with a noble Cathedral, and many interesting monuments of the past. Another day of travel through a region filled with manufactories of iron, and cities and towns which are thriving and busy, and rapidly growing in wealth and population, and we come to the borders of Scotland, where we rest for the night. We wonder not that the Englishman is fond of his country. We love to think that with him we have a common interest and origin. We can respond Amen to the prayer that daily goes up from thousands of hearts, "God save the Queen." Every step we have taken calls us back to a mighty and wonderful past, and points to a noble future. Her institutions, and her government, bear the mark of strength and stability. Her people are free. Royalty as it is now understood, is the very opposite of oppression and tyranny. The evils which exist will disappear in the progress of a sound and liberal and enlightened policy.

May the time never come when we shall be aught but united with her in the bonds of a firm and enduring friendship. The Christian and Scholar will love England for all that she has been and all that she is. Demagogues may affect to despise and hate her, but men of thought, and who reverence the great and good, will remember that, amid the noblest lights of the Church and the State, England's sons have ever been found. Her Poets and Orators, her Heroes and Statesmen, her Sages, her Preachers and her Martyrs have made for themselves names which shall ever be remembered. Every field has a story—every hill and valley bears some witness to the past, and amid many a tale of shame and crime and oppression, also testifies to the power of truth, the light of the Gospel, the glory of the Church, and the Providence of God employed in her behalf.

XIII.

SCOTLAND, IRELAND AND HOME.

THE road which leads from Newcastle to Berwick, after passing for several miles in full view of the German Ocean, at length crosses the Tweed upon an immense bridge, resting upon twenty-eight arches, and rising one hundred and thirty-four feet in height, at the end of which lies the first town in Scotland. It was for long years the scene of many a fierce encounter during the border wars, until late in the fifteenth century it fell into the hands of the English. From its walls we had a noble view of the sea, and the Holy Islands, on which are the ruins of the ancient abbey. Leaving Berwick for the north, the road enters a country, every hill and valley of which is full of historic interest, while presenting, also, many a rich natural scene, heightened and improved by labor and taste. Not far from Berwick, is Halidon Hill, where the English defeated the Scotch in the year 1313. Beyond this is Norham Castle, situated upon a steep bank that overhangs the Tweed. Here is laid the opening scene of Sir Walter Scott's *Marmion*.

> "Day set on Norham's castled steep,
> And Tweed's fair river broad and deep."

Not far from this spot is the place where Edward I met the nobility of Scotland to settle the dispute concerning the Scottish crown, between Bruce and Baliol. Still beyond is the town of Coldstream, whence came the Coldstream guards, so famous in the wars of England. As we are whirled onward, we pass at brief intervals majestic ruins and lovely country seats, and noble old castles which have become celebrated by the traditions of the nation, or the songs of its poets. Yonder are the ruins of Roxburg Castle, and there a splendid abbey once stood, and the lofty walls yet tell the story of its beauty. Upon this rocky and conspicuous elevation stands the Smailholm Tower—the scene of Scott's Eve of St. John, and beautifully described in one of his introductory epistles to *Marmion*—

> "A barren scene and wild
> Where huge cliffs were rudely piled,
> But ever and anon between,
> Lay velvet tufts of loveliest green."

Passing onward a few miles we are dropped at the Melrose station, a short walk from the old abbey, one of the finest specimens of gothic architecture in Scotland. We are met at the depot by a Scotch friend who had come from Edinburgh to welcome us, and whose kind attentions we shall not soon forget. Our first visit was to the abbey. The church is the only part which now remains; the best preserved parts of which are the choir and transept. The whole of the vast fabric is profusely decorated with rich and elaborate carvings. Its windows and arches, and doorways, grand even in their ruins, tell us plainly, at what expense, and with what skill this edifice was reared. The abbey owes much of its celebrity to the Scottish bard who has in his Lay of the Last Minstrel described with all his wondrous power the beautifully fretted roof, and the whole scene that opens to the eye as we stand and look up at these massive ruins. In the church yard one of the finest views of the abbey is obtained, and this is the point from which the pictures of the ruins are usually taken. In wandering through the tombs that fill these grounds, I noticed a stone nearly 100 years old, on which was the following quaint but striking inscription:

> "The Earth goeth on the Earth,
> Glistening like gold—
> The Earth goeth to the Earth
> Sooner than it wold—
> The Earth builds on the Earth
> Castles and towers—
> The Earth says to the Earth,
> All shall be ours."

Leaving this scene we cross the Tweed by a slender suspension bridge to the home of our friend Mr. Elliott; the house having been built and once occupied by Sir David Brewster. The view from the grounds is one of great beauty, presenting a rural scene of hill and valley, mountain and stream, that impresses itself indelibly upon the mind. Here a warm and friendly Scotch hospitality awaited us, which we find ourselves still recalling with pleasure. Entering the family carriage after dinner, a delightful drive of two or three miles brought us to Abbottsford, the former home of Sir Walter Scott. The house is full of interest, as connected with the history of the great novelist. The relics which he had collected in his lifetime are worthy of notice, among which is a door from the old Tolbooth of Edinburgh, and the pulpit in which Ralph Erskine preached. In a small closet adjoining the study are the clothes which Sir Walter wore, and in a room overlooking the valley of the Tweed, he breathed his last. The family who now occupy Abbottsford are Roman Catholics, and most of the servants are of the same religious belief. But we found an old man in charge of some part of the grounds, who was a Scotch Presbyterian, and who was retained here partly from his long connection with the place and the family of Sir Walter. He spoke feelingly of the gradual extinction of the line; the only living grandchild being a young girl of feeble constitution, so that the probability was strong that the man whose great dream was to leave behind him a long line of descendants to preserve his name and family, would soon have none in whose veins his blood should flow. Leaving Abbottsford and the noble hills of Eildon behind us, we pass the ruins of Crichton Castle, described so beautifully in *Marmion*, and the stately tower of Borthwick Castle, and at length coming in sight of Arthur's seat, Anthony's chapel and Holyrood, are whirled through a tunnel and enter the station of Edinburgh, built in the valley between the new town and the old, and lying in the very heart of the city, and within a moment's walk of its principal hotels. I was at Edinburgh twice. On my first visit I thought it was the finest city I had yet seen, and when I had passed over my tour on the continent and returned to the spot, my impressions were only deepened, that for picturesque beauty, for wondrous historic interest, for its noble and commanding situation, for its strange contrasts of modern art with the grotesque architecture of other ages, Edinburgh is the most interesting city in Europe.

Delivering some letters from America, I found

friends whose warm-hearted hospitality I shall not soon forget. To Mr. Oliphant especially was I greatly indebted both for the enjoyment of pleasant intercourse with his family, and for his personal attentions as a companion in my explorations of the scenes in and around the city. Familiar as he was with every spot that history had made memorable, I found myself in the company of a christian gentleman, ready and willing to put me in the way of seeing all that was most of interest in Edinburgh, and who led me to places which I had wished above all others to see.

The city is surrounded by, and built upon hills, which add greatly to its beauty. If we take a position at the old palace of Holyrood, we find ourselves in a valley lying at the foot of several elevations. To the south and east is a mountain almost 800 feet in height, along which are the famous Salisbury Craigs, and around its base is the Queen's Drive. Just above us to the north lies Calton Hill, crowned with noble monuments to Stuart, Playfair, Nelson and Burns. Looking west the old town rises like a wedge with its thin end towards us, to the height of 400 feet, where stands the noble old castle of Edinburgh. On either side of this hill, the summit of which is the famous High Street, is a valley, that to the right being the Prince's Garden, formed by drying up an old loch, whose waters divided the city, and that on the left being the old Cow Gate. Let us enter the venerable palace of Holyrood, the ancient home of Scottish royalty. It is built in the form of a quadrangle, with a court 90 feet square in the centre. The apartments which have the most thrilling interest are those of Queen Mary, whose character and history have thrown a charm over the whole scene. Ascend the stairs and you enter the chamber of the unhappy Queen, which has remained unaltered since she left it. Yonder through that low door, half concealed by some old tapestry, is the cabinet out of which Rizzio was dragged and murdered, and the stains of his blood still darken the floor of the hall. On the north side of the palace are the ruins of the abbey of Holyrood, founded by David I in 1128. Charles I fitted it up as a chapel to give the Scotch a model of Episcopal worship, and was here crowned in 1633. James II arranged it for a Roman Catholic chapel, but in neither way would the stern Scotch Presbyterians be tempted to leave their chosen form of worship. The palace of Holyrood became the chief residence of Mary on her return from France. On the first Sunday after her arrival which was the anniversary of the massacre of St. Bartholomew, preparations were made to have mass in the Royal Chapel. When this was known, the city was everywhere raised against the attempt, again to introduce the Catholic faith into Scotland. It required the utmost effort on the part of some of the leading reformers to suppress the tumult. Among those who sternly resisted the attempted invasion upon the Scottish Creed was John Knox, who, in all his interviews with the Queen, showed that noble and manly courage which gained for him at his grave the eulogium, "Here lies he who never feared the face of man." It was in this Palace that the stern Reformer, when summoned before the Queen for his bold preaching against the errors of her reign and of the Papacy, so laid the truth home to her heart that she wept, and exclaimed, "Never was Prince handled as I am." Here, when she sent him forth to the ante-chamber where her ladies were in waiting, the earnest reformer began a religious admonition, of which these words are a sample. "O, fair ladies, how pleasing is this life of yours, if it would abide forever, and then that in the end you pass to Heaven with all this gay gear. But fie upon the Knave Death that will come whether we will or not, and when he has laid on his arrest, the foul worm will be busy with the flesh be it never so fair and tender; and the silly soul, I fear, shall be so feeble that it can neither carry with it gold, garnishing, glistening pearl nor precious stones." Who could curb a spirit like that of Knox? Who can wonder that to this day Scotland feels the results of his earnest and manly piety and zeal? Let us pass up from the Palace through the famous High street, presenting scenes utterly in contrast to these once witnessed here.

That old building with a projecting story and

14*

a stair-case winding up from the street, beneath which is a gin shop and a tobacconist's is the old home of *John Knox*, where he lived and died. Out of that window facing the Netherbow he used often to deliver his sermons to the crowd in the street. Over the door is the inscription in old English, "Love God above all and your neighbor as yourself." This house which, in the progress of improvement, was at one time devoted to destruction has been purchased by the Free Church and will henceforth remain a sacred relic of the reformer. Passing upward from this point we pause at the old Parliament House, now devoted to the judicial business of the nation. Upon the wall in the lower story hangs the original draft of the solemn League and Covenant into which Scotland entered against any invasion of her right to worship God according to the dictates of a conscience enlightened by His Word. Still beyond, there stands the venerable church of St. Giles, where Knox and his brethren preached the doctrine of the reformation. Here was the scene of the popular outbreak against the efforts of Charles I, to force the prelatic government and forms upon the Church of Scotland. It will be remembered that at the Reformation the Scotch Church assumed the Presbyterian order and discipline in harmony with the Continental Reformed Churches. Under this change the Catholic Cathedrals fell into hands of the Presbyterians, where they have ever since remained, and many of the Priests of the Catholic Church entered into their forms and doctrines. When, however, James came to the throne of England with his favorite motto, "No Bishop, no King," efforts were made to bring Scotland under the Prelatic form of Church order. The terrible massacres accomplished by the brutal Claverhouse and his ruffians were part of this mistaken attempt. When it was at one time regarded as certain that Scotland must yield and the Presbyterian government be destroyed, a Priest was appointed to preach in St. Giles' and read the new Liturgy prepared by Bishop Laud. As he was beginning his unwelcome and intrusive services, Jenny Geddes, who could bear it no longer, arose and taking up the stool on which she was sitting threw it at the Priest's head, exclaiming, "Will you say mass in my lug?" This was the signal for revolt which was followed by a renewal of the solemn League and Covenant, and ended in the entire conviction that England could never dragoon a Scotchman into worshipping God in any other way than that which his conscience would approve. In this Church I heard a sermon before the Lord High Commissioner of the Queen at the meeting of the General Assembly. The Earl, who is a member, and I believe an Elder of the Kirk of Scotland, came up from Holyrood in royal state and entered the throne pew with his officers and pages, while the Council, Judge Provost, &c., sat around the gallery in their robes of office and white wigs, surrounded by the officers of the Assembly in full dress. The Free Church whose exodus from the Established Church presented some noble evidences of earnest and self-denying attachment to principle, holds its meetings of assembly in a new and commodious building, nearly opposite the assembly Hall of the old Kirk. Passing still upward we reach the Castle, overlooking the city and occupying the summit of the hill. Its position is one of exceeding strength, three of its sides being precipitous and rising to an elevation of 393 feet. Here in 1093 died Margaret the Saxon Queen. Her chapel still stands in perfect preservation. Yonder, near that building, on an angle of the wall is a small lookout where Mary used to take her work and sit for hours in sight of that splendid scene that opened before her on every hand. In a chamber of the Castle her son first saw the light, and eight days after was let down that fearful precipice in a basket and carried to Stirling, where he was baptized by John Knox. Here too is the Ancient Regalia of Scotland, the Crown, the Sceptre and the Sword. Retracing our steps and recrossing the portcullis and esplanade, we turn by the way of High Street to a bridge which crosses the deep valley known as Cow Gate.

Passing down the grass market to an open square, we pause at the spot where the Covenanters were hung for their adherance to the principles of the Church of Scotland. Ascending from this point we enter the old churchyard of Gray Friars. Here the solemn League and Covenant was signed, and yonder monument marks the graves and honors the memory of the Covenanters who fell victims to prelatic power and intolerance. Retracing our steps we cross High Street, and standing for a moment on the bridge, which connects it with the new Town, look down upon the scene beneath and around us. There at the entrance of this valley is the Station of the North British Railway. Between this and the next bridge is the market, and beyond that the beautiful terraces of the Princes' gardens. Behind us rise the tall and antique houses of the old Town, above which we see the spires of the Free Church and the Assembly Hall of the Kirk of Scotland, and the venerable tower of St. Giles. Before us lies Calton Hill with its monuments and the modern and beautiful structures of the new city. Entering Princes street we have a fine view of ancient Edinburgh from Holyrood to the Castle. One side of this street only is built up, the other opening to the beautiful gardens which occupy the place of the old loch. Here stand the superb monument of Sir Walter Scott, and the National Gallery, a beautiful building of the Ionic order, built as a school of design, and for the exhibition of works of art.

Passing northward, we come into a broad and magnificent avenue filled with tasteful buildings squares, fountains, and statues. Beyond this we descend again toward a romantic valley in which stands a fountain known as St. Bernard's Well, and through which flows a small stream called the Water of Leith. If now we enter a carriage and turn eastward, passing across to High street, and then down toward Holyrood, through the lower suburbs of the town, we soon emerge into the country, and whirling along the Queen's drive look up toward Arthur's seat and Salisbury Craigs, and ascending that beautiful eminence obtain a magnificent view of hill and valley, and sea, and city, and hamlet, which make up the scenery of Edinburgh. Yonder are the ruins of Craigmiller Castle, where the Earl of Mar was imprisoned, and where Queen Mary often made her home. At our feet lies a romantic loch, and as we pass onward we find another beautiful sheet of water wholly embosomed in hills. Turning northward we see the Frith of Forth, with Leith and Granton, and the old fishing village of New Haven, whose women, in their quaint dresses, form one of the curiosities of the Edinburgh markets. Yonder by that pile of stones (Mushet's cairn) which we are passing, Effie Deans, the heroine of the "Heart of Midlothian," used to meet the ruffian Robertson. That low ruin to the left is St. Anthony's Chapel, and still beyond, as we approach the town from the circuit of the Queen's drive, is the cottage of the old Laird of Dumbidykes and the home of Jeanie Deans, from whose garden we pause to pluck a flower, as a souvenir of the place.

But time would fail to speak of Edinburg as its intense interest demands. There is the University, where some of the noblest minds of Scotland have labored. Here splendid hospitals rise as monuments of the wealth and benevolence of former citizens. At every turn some object meets the eye which is connected with thrilling memories of the past.

In this city, as the heart of Scotland, was the great question of religious freedom decided. It was Knox, and Hamilton, and the noble sons of Scotland, who showed to England and the world that no power could bind the conscience, or enslave a people whom the truth had made free. And Scotland, England, and America are feeling to-day the blessed results of that great battle which was there fought, in which intolerance and bigotry were made to yield to men who loved and valued the liberty of the gospel. Before leaving Edinburg, I cannot avoid an allusion to her preachers. Would to God our whole Church was filled with such men as I heard at St. Giles', at the hall of the Free Kirk, and at the church of Dr. Guthrie. Their preaching was not flash and glitter, and wild attempts to produce a sensation at all hazards, but earnest, pungent, faithful exhibitions of the gospel. And crowds listened to them, with serious and fixed attention. A Sabbath in Edinburg affords a strange contrast to that on the continent. All business is suspended; its streets are quiet as the country, and on every hand, as the church bells are ringing, may be seen throngs of worshippers with their Bibles in their hands, making their way to the house of God. The contrasts of virtue and vice are startling here, and appear more appalling, because seen in a land where virtue and order and piety predominate. It is natural that they who are vicious in such a community should surpass those who sink into crime under circumstances less favorable to good morals. But we must hasten to finish our view of Scotland. Taking the cars for the north, an hour's ride brings us to Stirling. Leaving the train, and turning up the rough and steep streets which lead to the castle, we are rewarded with one of the noblest views in Scotland. On the castle grounds, a fine company of Scotch Highlanders are undergoing their morning drill, to the shrill music of the bagpipes. As we approach the old palace, we pass under the window from which the Earl of Douglass was thrown, after his assassination by James II. In yonder armory stands the pulpit of John Knox, and here he baptized the infant son of Mary. Ascending the walls of the castle, we look out upon a scene of almost unparallelled beauty and interest.

To the west rise the noble Highlands of Ben-Lomond, Benvenue, and Benledi. To the east wind the lovely waters of the Frith of Forth, bordered by fertile fields and meadows, and beneath us sinks away from our feet the stupendous precipice upon which the castle stands. Casting our eye southward, we see the valley and the green hillock where tournaments were often held, and beyond this, about two miles, is the illustrious battle-ground of Bannockburn, where Robert Bruce, with 30,000 men, met and overcame Edward II with 100,000 soldiers. But we cannot pause amid these recollections. Here around this ancient church, lingers many a glorious memory of Scotland's heroes. That noble statue is of John Knox, and that is the monument of Melville. And here is one on which stands an angel with a scroll, on which is inscribed Isaiah 40: 27—30; and then is added "Margaret, Virgin-martyr of the ocean-wave, with her like-minded sister Agnes. Scotia's daughters, earnest scan the page and prize the flower of grace blood bought for you.—Psalm 9: 19." On the reverse is "Margaret Wilson, of Slenvernock." This is the touching memorial of a young Christian, who died a martyr to her faith, and a victim of prelatic arrogance and bigotry in the time of James II and Claverhouse. For her simple adherence to the Presbyterian Church, she was tied to a stake at low water-mark, and overwhelmed by the returning tide.

Passing away from these scenes and associations, we resume our seats in the cars for Callander and the Trossachs, following the route which Scott has immortalized in his beautiful poem of the Lady of Lake. At Callander we take seats in an open stage, and are soon in the midst of the most romantic scenery. In the northwest rises the majestic head of Benledi. On our left the river Leith winds through a lovely valley, bordered by the woodland slope of the hills that rise on either hand.

Skirting the border of the beautiful river Venachar, we reach Coilantogle Ford, to which spot Roderick Dhu conducted Fitz James, and where, having fulfilled his promise, he exclaimed,

> "See! here all vantageless I stand,
> Arm'd like thyself with single brand,
> For this is Coilantogle's Ford,
> And thou must keep thee with thy sword."

At this point Loch Venachar opens before us with its varied scenes of beauty. Passing onward, we leave on our right hand a collection of rude Highland huts, the first stage of the bearer of the fiery Cross of his Clan, the blazing symbol of war and death.

> "Duncraggan's huts appear at last,
> And peep like moss-grown rocks half seen,
> Half hidden in the copse so green."

Still beyond, is the Brig of Turk, and then the lovely Loch Achray, and then as we hasten onward, we reach the Trosachs, where a scene of wondrous beauty and romance awaits us. They form a series of mountain gorges, made up of—

> "Crags, knolls, and mounds, confus'dly hurled,
> The fragments of an earlier world."

The whole scene is one of interest and beauty—

> "So wondrous wild the whole might seem
> The scenery of a fairy dream."

Here is the spot where the horse of the gallant Fitz James fell and died; and yonder opens before us the lovely Loch Katrine. A fairy-like steamer has returned to take us on board, and as we pass a wooded promontory the whole lake bursts upon our sight. Here the fair Ellen first saw the Knight of Snowdoun. There is her island—

> "Where for retreat in dangerous hour,
> Some chief had framed a rustic bower."

And yonder rises Benvenue. And as we sail onward by cliff, and forest, and island, and hill, we find ourselves again re-peopling these scenes with the rude clans of the Highlands, and listen for the echoes of the song with which their leader was welcomed—

> "Hail to the chief who in triumph advances,
> Honored and blest be the evergreen pine,
> Long may the tree in his banner that glances,
> Flourish the shelter and grace of our line."

Resting for the night at Stronachlachan Hotel, we rise early that we may ascend one of the lofty hills that overlook the lake, and pluck a bunch of heather from its summit.

Resuming our route by stage, we pass through the wild and desolate region where Rob Roy had his haunts, and see the hut where Helen M'Gregor was born, and reaching at length the highest elevation on our route, descend by the side of a rushing torrent to the margin of the far-famed Loch Lomond. This lake is justly the pride of Scotland, with its beautiful islands, its bold headlands, and its lofty mountains. That vast mass of rocks, with an opening scarcely visible, is Rob Roy's cave; and yonder is a rude pulpit where the people often gather for worship in the open air. As we pass on, Ben Lomond rises 3,192 feet above the sea, and on every hand are wild and bare mountains and cliffs, whose deep shadows rest gently upon these now peaceful waters.

At the foot of the lake the cars are awaiting our arrival, and, whirling us on towards the Clyde, we look up at Dunbarton Castle, where Wallace was a prisoner, and whose commanding elevation makes it one of the landmarks of the river; and then, turning upwards towards Glasgow, we are, in an hour's time, landed in the very heart of the city. Glasgow, while it does not possess the historic interest or the wild romantic beauty of Edinburgh, is yet greatly its superior in commercial importance. It bears every mark of a prosperous and growing city. The modern part of the town is beautifully laid out, and built up with substantial dwellings and churches. One of the noblest antiquities is the venerable Cathedral, now used for worship by a congregation of the Established Kirk. In one of its vaults is laid the scene of the mysterious meeting between Rob Roy and Osbaldistone. Its interior presents a fine specimen of Gothic architecture. Just across a ravine, through which flows a small stream, and over which is thrown the Bridge of Sighs, is the Necropolis, one of the finest cemeteries in Europe. Upon the summit is the noble monument and statue of John Knox, and scattered over the sacred enclosure are the statues of many of Scotland's distinguished men. Every part of Glasgow shows life, and energy, and industry. The old parts of the city, with their close and narrow streets, are densely populated, chiefly by the lower classes, among whom the prevailing fashion of both sexes seems to be bare feet. I think it safe to say, here can be seen more women without shoes or stockings than in any other city in Europe.

The scenery around Glasgow is beautiful, as, indeed, it would be difficult to find a point in Scotland where it is not. Taking the cars southward, and skirting Ayrshire, with its gentle hills and valleys, and the home of Burns —now made ever memorable by his genius and his song,—we pass on towards Dumfries, to spend a day in the midst of scenes and friends, which will long dwell in our hearts. One must go to Scotland to fully understand what is meant by a Scotch welcome. We found it in Dumfries. A single note of introduction opened to us the warm greetings and kindness of Rev. Dr. Wallace and his family, with whom we spent the last day we were to be in Scotland, and introduced us to such scenes as Burns describes in his " Cotter's Saturday Night:"

"From which Auld Scotia's grandeurs rise."

We were delighted with Dumfries. Every

way we turned, we met with some object of interest. Here Burns lived, and in yonder churchyard, just opposite the manse, is his tomb, with a beautiful bas-relief of the poet at the plough, from which the genius of Scotland is calling him away. Here, too, in that venerable church-yard, are the tombs of many a martyr who died for the faith. Over yonder bridge, across the Nith, lies Maxweltown, on whose bonny braes lived Annie Lowrie, the heroine of a pleasant Scotch song. The Solway, which is at times fordable, and then navigable, and on whose beautiful banks we are now riding, brings to our minds the young Lochinvar, and his words to the father of his fair lady:

"I long loved your daughter—my suit you denied;
Love flows like the Solway, but ebbs like its tide."

By the side of yonder lovely stream are the ruins of an ancient monastery, and the scene just there is one of picturesque beauty, that causes it to dwell distinctly in the memory.

But we must bid farewell to these scenes and to Scotland. A short ride brings us to Gretna, where for years the famous blacksmith united the runaway couples from England, but whose occupation is gone since the new law regulating marriages. The train hurries onward, and we are borne away with sad hearts from the land of heroes and of genius, and the home of liberty and a pure faith. We look back upon that glorious country, and heartily exclaim, "God bless Scotland for all that she has been and all that she is." Who cannot love the land of Wallace and Bruce, of Knox and Melville and Moray, of Scott and Burns, of Chalmers and M'Cheyne? Who will not honor a nation whose sons have distinguished themselves in the strife for liberty and truth, in the walks of science and literature, in the State and Church? And when from her hills and valleys, her cities and hamlets, her children come to the shores of the Western Republic, they shall find a brother's welcome from those who have learned to love and value that freedom whose battles were fought in Scotland amid the scenes of the Reformation, and whose institutions are best typified in the Church for whose order and faith that people contended with an earnestness that nothing could successfully resist.

But we must pass away from these scenes. Midnight brings us to Liverpool—to our old pleasant quarters at the Victoria Hotel. We spent a Sabbath there, and in our lack of information respecting churches, selected from the directory the Oldham Street Scotch Church, knowing that we should have sound doctrine, whether preached with eloquence or not. We were not disappointed, and listened to a faithful and earnest discourse from the pastor, Rev. Mr. Forfar, by whose invitation I occupied the pulpit in the afternoon, and with whom I attended a children's meeting in the evening, and was greatly delighted with their familiarity with the Bible and Catechism—the two books on which a Scotch Presbyterian is brought up, and which have much to do with his character and steadfastness to the faith.

Liverpool, while it is a city of great importance as a commercial centre, has but little to interest the traveller beyond its magnificent docks and business arrangements. A little out of the city there is, however, a Zoological Garden, which, in the summer season, is a favorite resort. An hour's ride in the cars brings us to Chester, an ancient and venerable town, with a magnificent cathedral of great antiquity. Passing westward, we are skirting the wild mountains of Wales, and looking out upon the ever changing beauties of that region. The celebrated Menai Bridge, now, however, wholly outdone by the new Victoria Bridge at Montreal, we pass on this route, and then hurrying on by the sand-hills of Anglesea, we reach Holyhead, where large works are now in progress for the improvement of the harbor. A rough passage of six hours, with a cabin full of passengers in every stage of sea-sickness, brings us to Kingstown, whence we are carried into Dublin by the cars, and are soon at a hotel spending our first night in Ireland.

Dublin deserves all that is said of it as a fine city. Few streets in Europe can rival its far-famed Sackville street, with its noble monuments, its substantial houses, and its broad pavements and side-walks. Its university, its hospitals, its various churches, and public edifices, are finely built, and on every side there is an air of wealth, and taste, and comfort, which is exceedingly pleasant and attractive. We took a short but delightful excursion down into the county of Wicklow, filled with scenes of exquisite beauty, and although strangers, we found ourselves in pleasant converse with that model of his kind, an Irish gentleman. It was amid the scenes of this county that Moore wrote his beautiful song, "The Meeting of the Waters."

Retracing our steps, we enter the cars for Cork, and are taken through the very country from which are imported the largest class of the Irish population that reach our shores. Many a long and dreary moor is passed, with peat-bogs and Irish mud-cabins, with the very cows, and pigs, and chickens, and half-naked children, and bare-footed women, and men with pipes, and shillalahs, and brogans, that we find squatting upon the outskirts of our cities—at length finding their way to our polls and public offices. Emerging from this region, which is not well calculated to impress one favorably with Ireland, we come out into scenes whose striking contrast doubtless adds to their beauty. Down in yonder lovely valley, with swelling hills beyond, stands the far-famed Blarney Castle, in whose tower is the stone which imparts eloquence to the tongues of all who kiss it. Every new scene, as we now hasten onward, has some fresh charm, and makes us regret that we cannot linger amid so much that is picturesque and beautiful.

But here is Cork, and these crowds that we see around, are unmistakably Irish. And so is the company on the steamer to Queenstown, even to the woman who sells us a pint of plums, with the very accent and look of the orange-women that offer us their commodities at the wharf and railroad stations at home. We are charmed with the exquisite beauty of the river down which we are sailing. The eye is engaged every moment with the opening glories of some new scene, with island, and headlands, villas of exquisite taste, and well-cultivated farms, and hills crowned with broad-spreading trees, and cottages which stand beneath them. At Queenstown we have a noble harbor sheltered by two islands, and which is now yearly becoming more and more important to the commerce of Ireland. We were detained here a day beyond our time, and after looking over every part of the town, tried to get a sight of the country by means of an Irish jaunting-car, a one-horse vehicle, the very reverse of an omnibus, placing the passengers back to back, with their feet over the wheels. We would advise nervous, timid, and *sulky* persons to keep out of such a conveyance. As to the first of these, there is every apparent probability that as the driver spins round a corner at full speed, the natural law of centrifugal motion will send the luckless passengers on to the side-walk or down the hill, while as to the latter class, a jaunting-car is utterly and hopelessly inconsistent with all gravity, and a sour-vinegar-faced individual would seem as little at home in such a conveyance as a tragic actor in a farce. You cannot ride in one without laughing, and when you see one loaded down with merry Irish girls full of fun and good humor, or a company of Irishmen all alive with wit, jollity, and merriment, you have a most respectful appreciation of an Irish jaunting-car. But the time has come for us to bid farewell to these scenes. We regretted that we could not have seen more of Ireland. We saw enough to make us desirous to linger longer here. We wonder not that the Irishman loves his green isle. The poor, priest-ridden and ignorant people who come hither from that fair land, are not the class by whom we are to judge of its character. There is talent, and genius, and learning, and eloquence there, which command the respect of the world. May God continue His own work amid that people, until the sources of error and degradation shall be dried, and Ireland redeemed and regenerated, take her proper place in the scale of truth, and science, and liberty, and religion. But the gun of the steamer is echoing over the waters—the signal for our departure. We step on board a small tug-boat, and are soon set off upon the good ship *Kangaroo*, Captain Jeffray. A few hours, and we have passed by the beautiful and romantic coast of Ireland, with its cliffs, its deep caverns, its venerable ruins of castles and towers, and are rocking upon the swelling waters of the open sea, and the burden of our song is "Home Again."

It is but an act of common justice, as well as a most pleasing duty, to speak of the line of steamers in which we both went and returned. While the rates of fare are less by nearly one-half than those charged in the other lines to Europe, the accommodations are fully equal to theirs, and Captains Petrie and Jeffray, with their officers, are noble specimens both of sailors and gentlemen, and know well how to make their passengers comfortable and happy. We found on the *Kangaroo* a large company, with the usual variety of characters met with on a steamer. Among them were my young friend Mr. Prime, from whom I had parted at Lake Luzerne on his way over the Alps, and the Irish delegation, Drs. Edgar, Dill, and Wilson, who, after a successful visit to our country, have returned home in the *Edinburgh*, to which vessel Captain Jeffray had been transferred.

Our passage homeward was the entire reverse of the outward bound. Head-winds, heavy seas, severe gales, close-reefed top-sails, storm stay-sails, and such like nautical phrases, descriptive of rough weather, found their way almost daily into the log-book. I had always wished to see a storm on the Atlantic, and I confess when I got into it, I heartily wished myself out of it.

It is a wild and awful scene, a stupendous evidence of the majesty and power of Him who holds the waters in the hollow of His hand. Gradually, as the wind freshens and hauls around into the stormy quarters, the ship is put in trim for the battle of the elements. High up upon the masts, and hanging out upon the spars that are already tracing long segments of circles against the sky, the hardy sailors are engaged in reefing the sails, and making all close and tight. As the wind increases, the spars are swung round toward it to offer as little resistance as possible to its awful power. And now you can do nothing but watch and wait for the issue. Steadily and firmly the great heart of this iron monster keeps up its pulsations, and the ship without a sail nobly breasts the foaming billows. As the storm advances, the ocean rises under its fury, until the waves and the gale are at their height. As the eye glances across this wild and fearful waste of waters, it looks like some Alpine scene, when the wind catches up the spray, like drifting snow, and bears it across the sea and drives it over the ship, and sends it flying in thick scuds above the spars of the vessel.

And then as you stand and watch the motions of the ship, it seems as if she were instinct with life, and struggling like a living being amid that war of elements. As for a moment she rises upon the top of a wave, she seems to pause and tremble as she looks towards that chasm into which she is to descend, and where gradually she settles down, and as you look above you at the dark waves which surround you like a vast wall, you are so subdued and attracted by the sublimity and grandeur of the scene, as to lose all sense of fear in emotions of wonder and admiration. But let us go below.

You pass in the companion-way a group of miserable-looking objects, whose faces indicate the last and most hopeless stages of sea-sickness. Waiters are busy supplying the demand for brandy, oat-meal gruel, lemons, and all the various prescriptions for the invalids. Unhappy individuals who look as if their last friend had gone, are staggering to the side of the ship for purposes too well known to need a description. Occasionally, as the vessel reels and pitches, the crowd are thrown promiscuously together, and they are only able to recover themselves, when a second lurch tumbles them as unceremoniously into another pile of extemporaneous acrobats.

In the cabin things are no better. A ghastly and miserable group are trying the same hopeless experiment of keeping and sitting quiet. Waiters are busy preparing the tables for dinner. Sometimes, as a sea breaks over the vessel, there is a crash of falling crockery and a rush of water through the sky-lights and companion-way, and a momentary pause as the ship quivers and shakes, and then hurries on again in her noble struggle with the winds and waves. At length the eight bells strike, and then the steward's bell sends its summons for dinner. With many the steam and odor are enough. Others stagger their way to the table. It requires no little skill to adjust matters there to any degree of comfort and safety. Soup plates are tilted up on the edges of the guards and then held carefully with the left hand. Meats and gravies are watched with a jealous eye, and unless held in their place by main strength, when an unlucky lurch of the ship happens, will be deposited in the lap of some luckless passenger, and, even with the utmost diligence, the whole service of the table often indicates an evident inclination to jump over on to the floor. A hungry man in a storm at sea is, on the whole, a pleasant specimen of one in the pursuit of a dinner under difficulties. But the hour for sleep comes, and we must enter those close and restricted apartments called state-rooms. You may imagine what evolutions are essential to reach your berth, especially if it happens to be on the windward side of the ship. You attempt to draw off a boot; just as it has started you are compelled to dance a reel across the room, and finish by pitching into your neighbor's berth head first. Recovering yourself, and waiting until the ship is on an even keel, you finish your boot and attempt your coat. Just as your arms are pinioned by your sleeves behind you, another lurch breaks open your door, tears away your trunks and carpet-bags, and sends you spinning against the side of the room. When at length, bruised and breathless, you are ready to enter your berth, you have to climb up the sides of a movable precipice, and, waiting for a favorable moment to reach your bed, spring into your place of rest. During this operation, you will probably raise several new phrenological developments upon your head, and nearly dislocate a shoulder, besides receiving several minor contusions, which, anywhere but on ship-board, would need the aid of a surgeon. But if you think your troubles are now over, you are sorely mistaken. You find a most frightful inclination of your body to follow the tendencies of gravitation, and must call the steward to box you in with a lee-board, against which you are rolling with every lurch of the ship. And then as the vessel heaves and pitches, you are standing alternately on your heels and your head, and rolling like an infant in its cradle, from the right to the left, from your back to your face. Thus the night is passed, and the morning brings a renewal of your last evening's troubles, ten times more aggravated, especially if you feel obliged to go through the operation of shaving. With such an experience, your first wonder will be how any sane man, who has a cottage anywhere on land, and enough to feed and clothe him, can ever choose the sea for his home. And your second reflection will be, that if any class of men deserve the respect and sympathy and prayers of the world, it is the hardy sons of the sea.

But pleasant weather comes, and the sick ones crawl out upon deck, and the perils and discomforts of the storm are forgotten in the invigorating air and the splendid scenes of the ocean. All kinds of amusements are tried. A few wits publish a paper; others, who are musically inclined, entertain a group upon the deck, or in the cabin, with all kinds of songs, from "A Life on the Ocean Wave," to "Widow Machree," or "Vilikins and his Dinah." Others, walk the deck or play at shuffle-board, or checkers, and fill up the intervals of time with eating, drinking, and sleeping. Our evenings are varied by concerts and lectures, in which last Dr. Edgar and his brethren, and the Rev. Mr. Scott, of the Episcopal Mission to Africa, entertained our company with much valuable information. The monotony of our voyage was somewhat varied by a visit to Halifax, where we had put in to replenish our coals, which had nearly been exhausted by our protracted passage.

On the Sabbath, religious services were held—the Captain reading the Episcopal liturgy, and one of the clergymen preaching a sermon. We shall not soon forget the pleasant scenes of the three Sabbaths we spent on our voyage homeward—the serious attention which was bestowed upon the religious exercises, and the delightful meetings for prayer, in which so many united, and by which they were gladdened and refreshed.

The last Sabbath evening was one of special interest. It was spent in narrating and listening to the history of the revivals in America and Ireland, and although the storm without was beating fiercely upon us, in that cabin a cheerful and happy group of Christians were committing themselves and all they held dear, to God—and speaking and hearing of all His mighty acts of grace and love. The next day brought us in sight of home, and never did it appear so lovely as when we steamed up the harbor of New York after an absence of four months and a-half, and never did we feel more loudly called upon for devout gratitude to God than when we saw upon the shore a part of our own family, and heard, ere yet we reached the land, that parents and children, the loved ones from whom we had been separated, and after whom had gone forth many a longing wish and earnest prayer, were safe and well. None but he who has thus been separated from all that make up for him the precious name of home;

who has dreamed of the absent amid ocean storms, and in foreign lands; who has sometimes feared that sickness or death might, peradventure, be busy with their fearful work around his fireside, and who has approached the shores of his native country with a beating and anxious heart, can tell the joy and gratitude which we felt as we folded to our hearts our children, and knew that all was well.

I have thus endeavored to reproduce the scenes through which it has been my privilege to pass. If I have afforded profit or pleasure to any; if any have been led to love and value America the more, and to feel, as I do, that it is the best and dearest land on which the sun shines; if I have induced any to think more kindly, and with a warmer sympathy for the sailor; if I have been the means of adding in any mind to its stores of knowledge, or have in the least degree promoted the interest and prosperity of this Church to which, with God's aid, my constant and earnest efforts shall be given, my labor has not been in vain. Let me but express the hope that, by God's grace, all who now hear me may have Christ for their pilot over this great ocean of life, until they shall find rest in that haven where there are no more storms, and in that land where there shall be no more sea.